FAMULUS DE EPISCOPO

An Adjutant's Manual

FAMULUS DE EPISCOPO
An Adjutant's Manual

By

Bishop Arnulfo A. Peat, Jr.

Elder David J. Stevens, Sr.

CECO Publishing

© Copyright 2013 CECO Publishing

All Scripture quotations are taken from the Authorized King James Version of the Bible unless otherwise stated.

Famulus de Episcopo:
An Adjutant's Manual

5210 South Cowan Road, Columbia, MO 65205
Mailing: P.O. Box 1523
　　　　Columbia, Missouri 65205
Website: www.cecofellowship.org/School-of-Adjutancy.html
Email: schoolofadjutancy@cecofellowship.org

ISBN: 978-0-9836336-3-1

No part of this publication may be reproduced, stored in a retrieval system, or transmitted, in any form or by any means, electronic, mechanical, photocopying, recording, or otherwise, without the written prior permission of the authors.

Contents

INTRODUCTION BY THE AUTHORS v

Chapter One	Discipleship: Journey of a Lifetime	13
Chapter Two	What is an Adjutant?	21
Chapter Three	The Servant Ministry of Adjutants	29
Chapter Four	Episcopal Orders	41
Chapter Five	Episcopal Insignia	45
Chapter Six	Ecclesiastical Vestments	51
Chapter Seven	Ecclesiastical Protocol and Etiquette	65

GLOSSARY OF TERMS 77

APPENDIX 83

ENDNOTES AND BIBLIOGRAPHY............................. 91

ABOUT THE AUTHORS 93

Introduction

We are currently living in a moment of time that society has filled with individuals that are focused and centered on themselves and their own personal agendas. Every decision they make concerning their life is out of a value system of self-preservation. Self-preservation is not connected to a greater work outside of an individual's personal interest and desires. Yet in the midst of this dominant cultural belief, the Lord is raising up men and women that have a love and desire to serve Him and His elect leaders. We are truly living in a time that the hearts of spiritual parents have turned toward their children and the hearts of the children toward their spiritual parents. Christians Equipping Christians for Outreach was the result of a father's heart turned towards his sons, and his son's hearts' turned toward their spiritual father.

Christians Equipping Christians for Outreach (CECO) Fellowship was birthed as part of a God-inspired vision given to Bishop Russell Larry Freeman. Through the collective efforts of his spiritual sons, manifestation of the original vision occurred in February 2008. These great men of God, under the leading of the Holy Ghost, performed the necessary tasks which were needed to open the door for Bishop Freeman and United Community Cathedral. In this, CECO serves as a help and an encouragement to other ministries within the Kingdom of God.

These sons, along with their spiritual father, became the founding fathers of CECO – Bishop Russell Larry Freeman, Bishop Lester Woods, Jr., Bishop Herman Dean Ware, Jr., Bishop Darrell Dewayne Luther, Sr., Bishop Arnulfo A. Peat, Jr., and Overseer Todd F. Robinson. In August 2009, CECO's Fathers unanimously elected Bishop R.L. Freeman as Presiding Prelate.

During the formative years of CECO Fellowship, it became clear that we would ascribe to an episcopal polity, a form of church governance, due to the nature of our work and the vision of our presiding bishop. This form of governance required CECO's leadership to develop and embrace the habits of the episcopal form of governance to meet our needs. The Apostle Paul admonished the Church to "Let all things be done decently and in order." The fellowship adopted liturgical practices of the Universal Church and established habits that are unique to this fellowship. Liturgical practices of the fellowship can be seen in our celebration services, liturgical vestments, and episcopal consecrations.

Within CECO, it was determined that there was a need for a corps of individuals well versed in areas of liturgy, ethics, protocol, Episcopal traditions and vestments; who will provide stability and order during the fellowship's gatherings. This corps would be called upon to assist in shaping the Fellowship by promoting uniformity and understanding of proper protocol. It was determined that those serving as adjutants and armor bearers to bishops needed a central location from which to receive guidance on policy, training, mentoring and a "voice" of consistency, so that they can assist their episcopal leader in promoting order in the Fellowship.

Famulus de Episcopo: An Adjutant's Manual was written to equip adjutants in the habits of CECO's Fellowship, so that their appointment will be fruitful and productive. The title we have chosen is translated "servant of the bishop", this is not to suggest that adjutants serve only consecrated bishops, but that we serve the leaders of the church. The manual is designed to address the disciplines of the appointment and the pragmatic functions of the adjutant's service to leadership and the fellowship in which they serve. Commitment and preparation serve as fundamental pillars for the adjutancy. These pillars cannot stand without a solid foundation, an unwavering passion and commitment to serve Christ. This manual will address the following subjects that we have found relevant to the work of adjutant in Christians Equipping Christians for Outreach and the Universal Church:

- Discipleship
- What is an Adjutant
- The Servant Ministry of Adjutants
- Episcopal Orders
- Episcopal Insignia

- Ecclesiastical Vestments
- Ecclesiastical Protocol and Etiquette

We pray that your ministry is richly blessed and enlightened by the contents of this manual as it serves as a guide for the governance of CECO's adjutancy and its implementation to aid local fellowships.

Chapter I

Discipleship:
A Journey of a Lifetime
By Bishop Arnulfo A. Peat, Jr.

Seth Godin's book entitled "Tribes: We need you to lead us" addresses the need for leaders that are committed to a specific group of people with specific needs. A tribe is defined as *"a group of people connected to one another, connected to a leader, and connected to an idea"*.[1]

This concept of "tribe" is essential as we proceed in the reading and implantation of this adjutancy manual. Godin's definition of tribe is centered on the word and/or principle of being connected. Why would we read and study an adjutancy manual unless we share a passion of this nature to serve? We must be connected to our leaders, and we must be connected to an idea, which can be interpreted as vision. We serve because of a commitment to a living God, a living savior. This ministry requires individuals that are committed to men and women that carry an apostolic mantle and who are committed to an apostolic mandate – The Great Commission.

[19]Go ye therefore, and teach all nations, baptizing them in the name of the Father, and of the Son, and of the Holy Ghost: [20]Teaching them to observe all things whatsoever I have commanded you: and, lo, I am with you alway, even unto the end of the world. Amen. [2]

When one begins to build a core of individuals with the primary function of service to the episcopacy and those in senior leadership positions, one must have a clear understanding of what is going to be required of these individuals for their journey with their leaders. Preparation and commitment serve as the foundation of the adjutancy. The foundation built by preparation and commitment can only be established if individuals are willing to be a disciple and have an unwavering passion to serve Christ in all things. Discipleship is not

14 | Discipleship: Journey of a Lifetime

exclusive to the adjutancy, but it is required of all believers in the faith. Discipleship is *"the diligent and intentional teachings and practices that promote the lifelong lifestyle of becoming ever more like Jesus and reproducing the Christ-life in others"*.[3] The discipleship journey is very difficult, because the primary function or objective is transformation.

Adjutants and armor bearers find themselves in a unique position; some are a part of their leader's inner-circle or find themselves privy to their leader's intentions, actions, and their hearts desires. This position comes with a great deal of responsibility and accountability. Individuals looking in will see you as one of power and influence, because of your relationship with your apostolic leader. Those looking in will never see and experience the weight of the appointment. Adjutants and armor bearers are charged to cover their leader for the purpose of sanctifying the office their leader holds and protecting their leader's apostolic mantle. Because of the weight of your responsibility, one cannot be spiritually, emotionally, physically and intellectually undisciplined. Your appointment should be predicated on your character and its perpetual growth as a man or woman of God!

> *"If I take care of my character,*
> *My reputation will take care of itself."*
> *- D.L. Moody*

Discipleship is a lifelong journey that must be intentional to the believer. Believers must make a commitment to becoming Christ-like in their walk, while investing in the lives of others. Discipleship utilizes the disciplines of the faith for spiritual formation, which includes character development and it is through the utilization of the disciplines that we can grow closer in our relationship with our heavenly Father.

The Disciplines of the Faith are:

- ❖ Prayer
- ❖ Fasting

- ❖ Meditation
- ❖ Studying
- ❖ Solitude
- ❖ Submission
- ❖ Simplicity
- ❖ Service
- ❖ Confession
- ❖ Worship
- ❖ Celebration
- ❖ Guidance

These disciplines are valuable tools in our spiritual, physical, and intellectual growth as Christians. All of them are very important, but I will place emphasis on only a few of these disciplines. As adjutants and armor bearers, these disciples are essential in the development of our character. Our character is a virtue that will allow us to cover our leaders and embrace the weight of our appointment. The weight of our appointment should not be entrusted to novices and individuals with highly questionable character traits. These individuals will have been prematurely given access to the leader and their family, finding themselves unprepared for the task before them.

The intentional practices of the disciplines from a Biblical Worldview is a means of us receiving God's grace and become a recipient of God's transformational Power in our life.[4] God's grace and transformational Power is necessary for the transformation of the human and/or worldly presupposition. Francis A. Schaeffer suggests that presuppositions are the "basic way an individual looks at life, their basic worldview, the grid through which he sees the world," a person's presupposition establishes itself on an individual's perceived reality of truth.[5] An individual presupposition is "a grid for all they bring forth into the external world." It also provides us with the foundation of our values and the reasons for our decisions.[6] Presuppositions are learned behaviors we have embraced from others in our tribe or things we feed our inner man.

We defined discipleship as diligent, intentional teachings and practices that promote the lifelong lifestyle of becoming ever more like Jesus and reproducing the Christ-life in others. With this in mind, discipleship becomes an intentional methodology for character development or in other words becoming a recipient of God's transformational power to change our presuppositions, change our learned behaviors and replace them with His.

Damazio states that character is the inner life of man. An individual's character "will reflect either the traits of the sinful nature (being influenced by the world) or the traits of the divine nature (being influenced by the Word of God)".[7] A large part of an adjutant and armor bearer's preparation will come from their commitment to the practices of the disciplines.

The ultimate goal of an adjutant's commitment to the disciplines of the faith is more than just a transformed life, but a transformation that reflects the image of Christ and a strong relationship with our heavenly Father. The function of the disciplines is to move us toward this end. There are many Biblical disciplines, but we will briefly address **The Inward Disciplines**: meditation, prayer, and study and **The Outward Disciplines**: simplicity, submission and service. Adjutants and Armor Bearers that consistently practice these disciplines will know God's will for their life and will perform an honorable service in excellence for God's elect leaders.

The Inward Disciplines

We live in a society and/or culture that moves at a rapid pace. In the midst of this rapid pace: information, data, images, and messages are received through our senses. If these messages are not properly filtered, habits and presuppositions (learned behavior) will begin to take root in our lives. This is why the inward disciplines are vital to our spiritual growth, they serve as spiritual filters; allowing us to discern truth. In addition, the inward disciplines work to uproot and transform those presuppositions and habits of sin in our life, while establishing a sanctuary in the heart of man.

- **Prayer**

An adjutant must have a strong prayer life! A prayer life moves an individual into a perpetual dialog or communion with our heavenly Father. Foster suggests that the discipline of prayer brings us to a place of deep intimacy and fellowship with our creator.[8] In this place we find that prayer is life giving and transformative in nature. As we pray and commune with Him, God's grace begins to reveal our current conditions and sets us free from them. It is difficult to cover and/or intercede on your leader's behalf when you are preoccupied with hiding your sins from an all-knowing God. We must be intercessors at the highest level, so that ministry can go forth.

- **Meditation**

Meditation is designed to build the believer's capacity to hear God's voice and to obey His word. Spiritual understanding and revealed truth is facilitated by the Holy Spirit through the discipline of meditation. Adjutants' ability to be reflective is fundamental to their appointment and necessary for their spiritual growth. Meditation is a deep reflection on scripture verses or passages in a way that God's word becomes a living epistle that is applied to our heart, so that transformation can occur.

- **Study**

In order to nurture our spiritual growth that has been obtained through prayer and meditation, a commitment to become a lifelong learner is necessary. Study is the experience in which the mind is conformed to what the individual is studying, preferably God's word. Through the discipline of study, you will come to understand who God is and come to know the liberating power of God's truth. As an adjutant and/or armor bearer, you are not only required to study the Bible and sound biblical literature, but you must study the lives of individuals and particularly the lives of those you serve. In order to operate within this appointment with a spirit of excellence, the adjutant must study their leader's habits and know how they flow during time of ministry and outside times of service. In studying your leader's habits, it allows you to flow with them as they follow the leading of the Holy Spirit. The key to sustaining this level of ministry is the adjutant's consistency in prayer and meditation. It is the foundation to a heightened sense of spiritual discernment and service to your Episcopal leader.

The Outward Disciplines

As we undergo an inward transformation, we must not forget that the ultimate proof of transformation is an outward manifestation of what has transpired inwardly. The outward disciplines cultivate a social dimension of our spiritual life journey.[9] Without this dimension or outward manifestation, our spiritual pursuits will become self-centered; old habits or presuppositions are likely to return. Foster suggests that these Christian disciplines are inward realities that result in an outward life style.[10] In this section we will look at three disciplines: simplicity, submission and service. These disciplines can only be supported and manifested if the inward disciplines are established in your heart. If the inward disciplines are not established, the outward disciplines will become works and absent of God's grace.

- **Simplicity**

The discipline of simplicity is the practice of living a life without excess, greed and covetousness, as we grow closer to God and minister to the needs of others with a spirit of compassion. Life is filled with many distractions and/or pursuits that can prevent us from seeking the Kingdom of God and a single-hearted devotion to a living God and His work. The practice of simplicity will assist us in not becoming entangled with the things of this world. (Gal. 5:1) As adjutants, we must be free from the distractions that can prevent us from performing our appointed duties with a spirit of excellence. Juggling a family life, a regular job, and ministry obligations can be very difficult in of itself, but if we add additional distractions and/or pursuits, we will compromise in other areas of our life.

- **Submission**

The discipline of submission is one of the most abused and misused biblical principle. There are times that religion will use this discipline to place others in bondage or feed individuals with a sense of false obligations. The disciplines, when used properly will provide us with freedom and the ability to lay down our burdens. A life of submission "enables us to lay down the everlasting burden of needing to get our own way"[11] and build a capacity to trust God, His word and His will for our life. Submission allows us the freedom to value others and their individuality, because of our commitment to the call on our life.

- **Service**

The discipline of service naturally flows out of our love and relationship with our heavenly Father. Every believer is gifted to serve with their assigned spiritual gifts and talents. Adjutants have an extraordinary gift of service as long as their relationship with God is in order. If it is not in order, they move into a spirit of works and grudgingly serve the Man or Woman of God.

An adjutants and/or armor bearer's appointment can be a coveted position for the wrong reasons; for some, their interest is not to serve because of their love for a living God. Adjutants must develop a level of sensitivity to the move of the Holy Spirit. You must have this heightened sense of discernment to move with the Holy Spirit and submit to His leadership and authority. The disciplines of the faith and the Universal Church will allow adjutants to accomplish this task, have an inner peace and build a life of spiritual, mental, and physical strength for the journey before you.

Reflections

- Reflect on your level of commitment to the disciplines of the faith. As you reflect, consider which ones are you consistently practicing and strive in what areas do you fall short. Make a conscious effort to improve upon your commitment to these disciplines and pray for the guidance and strength of the Lord to aid your endeavors.

- As a disciple, at times you are the voice of your leader. Consider, do you have your leader's heart? Meaning; do you understand his vision and direction? Take some time to make sure that you can articulate your leader's vision and where he or she is going

Chapter II

What is an Adjutant?

Defining the Term:

Merriam-Webster defines an adjutant as; a staff officer in the army, air force, or marine corps who assists the commanding officer and is responsible especially for correspondence; one who helps: Assistant.[1] As we look at the role of the military adjutant, we will find much relation in that of the church adjutant.

Military Adjutant:

Today's military adjutant is responsible for carrying out and enforcing the intentions of the commanding officer (CO) as it regards policy and directives, and to represent those intentions in writing. To fulfill this purpose, the adjutant must understand commander's intent. Commander's intent briefly, is the overall end state of a mission or objective from the commander, it is what must be achieved by reputable and safe means. How this intent is carried out is wholly up to those under the charge of the commander. Because of this designation to put the commander's intent in writing, the adjutant must remain abreast of current policies and procedures in order to maintain order in any situation within his purview.

The adjutant also serves, at times, as an advisor to the CO in matters when advisement is requested; if not requested this advice is not freely given. This maintains order in the professional relationship between the adjutant and the commanding officer and serves to ensure that boundary in the relationship is never crossed.

(Take note: when advisement is given, it is provided in a manner that bespeaks of much humility and in a proper attitude. The adjutant by no means should feel, nor be led to feel, that he is "in charge", especially when advising the CO. It is the duty of the adjutant to carry out and enforce the directives and policies of the CO, not make his own.)

The military adjutant is a buffer to the CO and fields issues that are not necessary of the CO's immediate attention or action. As a buffer, the adjutant ensures all official correspondence is properly formatted and complete before presenting to the CO. This is not to say the adjutant decides what is and is not urgent enough to be brought to the attention of the commanding officer. Simply put, upon consulting the CO, the adjutant may be given leave to take care of some situations that are within his purview. In this regard, the present day adjutant is a manager of the schedule of the CO, maintaining strict adherence to appointments and keeping the CO abreast of necessary changes and requirements in policy. Through all of this, we can see that the military adjutant is policy writer, advisor, steward, filter/buffer, sounding board, scribe and clerk to his commanding officer.

The Church Adjutant Defined

How does this military position relate to the Servant-Ministry within the Pentecostal Church today? In 1971, while observing the need for someone to assist the Religious Leader of the denomination to which he belonged, Bishop Jesse Delano Ellis, II, created a job description for this need.[2] The term "adjutant" provided the foundation for this Office and from that, Bishop Ellis set about to develop a dress code for that denomination's bishops and clergy. In creating a standard among the clergymen of that Reformation, the Adjutancy within the Pentecostal Church was born. Because of this work and his identifying the need for and founding this ministry, Bishop Ellis is known as the "Father of the Adjutancy".

The church adjutant borrows more than the title from the military version of the same name and much of his structure is based upon the military example. The church adjutant is responsible for enforcing the intentions of the bishop in policy writing and is expected to be an example for all members of the church. To achieve this, the adjutant must similarly remain abreast of local as well as national church policies, customs and etiquette. It sometimes falls within the purview of the adjutant to draft letters of introduction, policy, proposals and other official correspondence on the behalf of the prelate.

Like the military, the church adjutant is a buffer for his bishop. In this capacity, he is expected to know the heart of his leader and be able to determine what needs to be brought to his immediate attention or what can wait. The adjutant sometimes speaks on the behalf of his bishop when that authority and grace has been granted. It is not that the adjutant would act exactly like the bishop in a certain regard, it is that the relationship has been established and the adjutant carries the heart and spirit of his bishop, thus his actions are trusted to represent his leader well.

There are of course elements we do not see in the military adjutant that in whom the church counterpart must be well versed; these elements are centered on matters of the Spirit. The church adjutant is intercessor, spiritual warrior, prayer partner and more in the service of and with his leader. To this end, it is imperative that the spiritual bond and relationship between bishop and adjutant be properly built so that the adjutant can be better equipped to assist his leader. This is especially seen during deliverance, spiritual warfare and intercession. However, in all of this, we cannot address Church Adjutancy without addressing the foundational concepts of servant-hood and discipleship.

The Adjutant as Minister and Servant

The adjutant is first and always a servant. His office of ministry is described as "chiefest among the servants of the *non*-Episcopally consecrated servants of Christ."[3] What that means is that the Adjutancy serves as example to all others as it pertains to willing Godly service, humility and protocol. It is to this office that all other servants are to look for guidance and strength in serving God's leaders. Just as Peter exhorts the elders to be "ensamples to the flock" (I Peter 5:3), the adjutant is to be an example to the presbytery.

It is from the twentieth chapter of the Gospel according to Matthew, taking emphasis from the 25th through the 28th verses, that the Adjutancy takes its charge. *"But Jesus called them unto him, and said, "Ye know that the princes of the Gentiles exercise dominion over them, and they that are great exercise dominion over them, and they that are great exercise authority upon them. But it shall not be so among you: but whosoever will be great among you, let him be your minister; And whosoever will be chief among you, let him be your servant: Even as the Son of man came not to be ministered unto, but to minister, and to give his life a ransom for many."*

We follow the servant example of Christ in this ministry and take our lead from him. From this passage of scripture, we take note of a couple of descriptive terms: minister and servant. The Greek word used here for minister is interpreted from *diakonos* meaning: an attendant.[4] This Greek term diakonos is also illustrated in Acts 6 when the first deacons were appointed. Peter instructs that the disciples look amongst themselves and find men "of good report, full of the Holy Ghost and wisdom." It is here, coupled with further examination in 1 Timothy 3:8-12, that we can find qualifications for service as a deacon, and an adjutant.

Back in Matthew 20, the word servant in this verse is interpreted from *doulos* meaning: bondservant, one knit or bound.[5] Therefore, in defining the term adjutant we see that he is a servant, bound in his service to God. It is worth mentioning here that the bondservant is bound not out of obligation, but out of love. In the Old Testament, it is recorded that servants would serve for six years and in the seventh, they would be freed. If in fact, as Exodus 21:5 illustrates, if the servant declares that he desires to remain in the service of his master out of his love for him, then he would be bound to him until the masters' death. Again, we want to emphasize that this lifetime of service is a willing choice. The adjutant honors God by serving and honoring his leader and is bound to do so by nature of the Office in which he operates. The functions of the adjutant (to be discussed in the following chapter) directly support this definition; what the adjutant does supports who he is, but does not define him.

Note: We are not honing in on specific terms pertaining to the function of the Adjutancy on purpose; the aim of this chapter is to define what an adjutant is, not how he functions in his identity. Sometimes the lines between existence and purpose are crossed

back and again and this is perfectly fine. It is because of the protean nature of being a servant that we must clearly define the term 'adjutant'.

From this we determine that the adjutant is an attendant and bondman to his God appointed leader. There are separate classifications of adjutants within the Fellowship; however, this teaching will serve to give a broad definition in a holistic view of the term "adjutant".

The Adjutant as Disciple

And Jesus, walking by the sea of Galilee, saw two brethren, Simon called Peter, and Andrew his brother, casting a net into the sea: for they were fishers. And he saith unto them, Follow me, and I will make you fishers of men. – Matthew 4:18-19

The term 'disciple' is found in the bible in various forms and on 274 occasions. It is translated from words like *mathēteuō* (math-ayt-yoo-o), *mathētēs* (math-ay-tes), or *mathētria* (math-ay-tree-ah) all meaning: to learn as a pupil.[6] The adjutant is primarily servant to his leader and secondarily pupil. As elders of the church, we are servant-leaders but as adjutants, we are servant-pupils. Therefore, not only does the adjutant serve, he learns from his leader for the purposes of: 1) being a better minister and 2) carrying on the work of the ministry. The Adjutancy is after all, a ministry of progression, but that is for another discussion.

In the thirteenth chapter of Matthew, Jesus is teaching the multitudes through a series of parables. Throughout the course of this recollection of history, we see the disciples asked a question, Jesus provided an answer and finally we see how Jesus verified understanding had been gained in the answer. This is an illustration of the many instances of their interaction as master and pupils.

The relationship Christ shared with his disciples is what we are to pattern the adjutancy after. The manner in which the disciples forsook everything and followed Christ is the ultimate representation of relationship between the bishop and his adjutant. Many of today's adjutants are not able to follow after this pattern, we have families, spouses, full time secular jobs (as sometimes do our prelates) and additional responsibilities may prevent that depth of relationship with, and commitment to our prelates. This does not, however, say that we are not to pattern ourselves after their example and strive for that level of relationship. The relationship between the adjutant and prelate should be a paramount concern for both parties. This relationship will serve as the foundation of the work between the two. Without relationship, there can be no connection in Spirit, which is vital to the successful adjutant's work.

CECO Adjutant

So after all those words, what is an adjutant? The scope of the Adjutancy is such that to restrict it to a series of a few words in definition would be to; perhaps limit this Servant-Ministry. The role of the adjutant greatly depends, as aforementioned, on the relationship between the adjutant and his leader. Nevertheless, as promoters of structure and order in the church, we will attempt to provide a definition: *an adjutant is a servant of the church who is well versed in protocol, worship and ecclesiastic ceremony, for the purpose of promoting order in the church and assisting the prelature in all ecclesiastical, ecumenical and Spiritual matters.*[7]

What is the Difference between the Armor Bearer and Adjutant within CECO Fellowship?

Firstly, let us point out that among the qualifications for adjutants in CECO, we maintain that adjutants must at a minimum, be ordained deacons. This is owing to the fact that the ordained deacon will possess basic Christian knowledge, sincerity in commitment to the Lord and have the spiritual authority necessary for basic service as an adjutant. This distinction is not to diminish the work or need of the armor bearer in any way; this distinction is simply a necessity for the protection of the leadership of the church.

This Servant-Ministry is one of progression meaning that the armor bearer, in all that he does, should strive to serve as an adjutant. The adjutant functions on a level that is more demanding clerically and spiritually than that of an armor bearer. The successful adjutant will have previously served as an armor bearer and through time, maturity, study, patience, much humility and the work of the Spirit, progression will be made. This is not to suggest that all armor bearers will one day serve as adjutants. If there is not a need for further adjutants within the church or territory, then none will be trained and appointed. Much like episcopates in the Fellowship, adjutants are appointed according to the need, not for the sake of simply having adjutants. Whether we are appointed as armor bearers or adjutants, one constant is that we are serving the Lord through serving our leaders. It is this that should be our focus, not our particular designation within the Body of Christ.

Further distinction between these Offices of servant-hood is the practice that those who do not enjoy the privilege of episcopal consecration generally utilize the assistance of armor bearers, reserving the use of adjutants to consecrated prelates. When further assistance is required due to the scope of work at hand, more than one adjutant to the bishop may be groomed and appointed to assist the Adjutant Chamberlain or serve on a rotational basis to that particular prelate. Additionally, the use of more than one armor bearer is an accepted practice should the need arise in the local assembly for a pastor.

Reflections

- Every Episcopal house must have structure and spiritual order. Structure and order come through protocol, policies, procedures and our awareness of them. The question simply is; do you know the protocol and policies of the house wherein you serve?

- Can you effectively articulate the heart of your leader to others?
  You must strive to establish and maintain the spirit of your leader in order to effectively articulate their heart.

Chapter III

The Servant Ministry of Adjutants

A. Introduction

While it may be that the Adjutancy is known mostly for its responsibility to assist in matters of liturgy, ceremony and the maintaining of order among the habit of presbyters, these activities are not primary among those serving. It is not the intent of this School to propose that these duties should be diminished or viewed as insignificant in any way, quite the contrary; there is a great need for uniformity and order in the Church. The primary focus of the adjutant is to his leader, firstly in covering his leader with much prayer and intercession and secondly, in assisting his leader in matters deemed appropriate to this office, which speaks to the clerical and more visible nature of the adjutant. It is with this primary focus in mind that we take our stance and begin this lesson as to why there is a need for the Servant Ministry of the Adjutancy. We exist not for the purpose of knowing who stands where in a processional, or when a prelate needs to remove his zucchetto during service; but we exist for the purpose of assisting the episcopacy in spiritual matters.

B. Why the need for this ministry?

"The adjutant who cannot cover his leader's weakness is of no use to that leader."
- Bishop H.D. Ware Jr.

It is the primary function of the adjutant to cover his leader; all other duties are secondary. The adjutant who holds to the idea or concept that his leader is "spiritually indestructible", will fail to fulfill his assigned purpose. While it is true that those we serve operate within the apostolic mandate of CECO, and with all the power, authority and strength of the Lord; we must realize that it is because of this work and this anointing that they will be under constant attack. Our leaders are

Generals and Colonels in the Lord's army and the enemy is targeting our officers!

The armor bearers of the Old Testament were expected to follow their leader in battle, fighting side-by-side with their leader and assisting in a very physical sense. (1Sam. 14:6-13; 1 Chronicles 10:1-5) This correlates to today's adjutant in matters of the spirit. The adjutant is expected to wage spiritual warfare on the behalf of as well as alongside his leader. Anything less and you have become just someone to pour a glass of water and carry a bible, which frankly, anyone can do. Shortly after being assigned as adjutant to my Bishop, he told me "I don't need you to carry my bible." Although I continue to do this, I took those words to heart and it was not until later that I began to realize what he was really telling me.

In the 26th chapter of St. Matthew, we see the distinct need for this servant ministry as illustrated by Jesus and his disciples. After the Passover meal, Jesus and his disciples went to a garden near Jerusalem called Gethsemane. It is here that Jesus separates himself, along with Peter, James and John, from the remainder of the disciples. It is not until they are alone, the three and Jesus, that Jesus exposes his weakness. The 37th verse reads *"And he took with him Peter and the two sons of Zebedee, and began to be sorrowful and very heavy."* This speaks to the nature of the relationship and trust shared between the adjutant and his leader. The adjutant will be privy to the more intimate needs and conditions of the leader and MUST keep those conditions in confidence while at the same time upholding them constantly before the Lord in intercession.

Jesus goes further to voice his condition by stating in the 38th verse, *"My soul is exceeding sorrowful, even unto death:"* It is obvious at this point, that Jesus is going through quite an ordeal. From his prayer we discover that Jesus is experiencing a conflict between his divinity and his humanity. The God in Christ would that he stand and endure, while waiting for his captors to come and fulfill his mandate as vicar, yet his humanity would have him flee and avoid impending pain and an agonizing death. This is where the adjutant is needed most, to lift up his leader in prayer and to war with him in the spirit, especially (not only) during times of trial or weakness.

Jesus instructs the three disciples closest to him to *"tarry ye here, and watch with me."* To tarry is of course to remain or stay in a given place, state or expectancy. The fact that Jesus said for them to watch <u>with</u> him shows that we are not expected to war alone, and neither should our leader. The disciples were to cover Jesus during this time, not for the purpose that God intervene and he escape his situation, but that he has the strength to endure and fulfill what God had for him.

> "And thou shalt bring in the table, and set in order the things that are to be set in order upon it;"
> - Exodus 40:4a

There is obviously a certain level of protocol, ceremony and order among all that we do in the Church. The uniformity in areas of habit and liturgy help to distinguish us as a functioning body as opposed to a mob of believers without purpose or direction. Generally speaking, the adjutant becomes the personal chamberlain to the bishop and assistants in ceremonial matters.[1] Further, adjutants are the visible interpreters of the Dress Code of the Church and as such, adjutants should always keep abreast of the Code so that they may be able to assist in determining the proper vestment for any given occasion.[2] This is but a brief and broad description of the function of the adjutant in the Church and is not intended to be all-encompassing.

C. Classification and Roles of the Adjutancy

"All adjutants are members of the Presiding Bishop's Apostolic Household. You serve the Lord by serving your leader(s) in office and you bring honor to Christ when you bring honor to His Bride, the Church. Your calling is an honorable one and must never be taken lightly."
- *Vocati Ad Ministrandum*, Archbishop J.D. Ellis

Firstly, let it be known that adjutants can be elected and appointed by a number of means; 1) selected by the Presiding Prelate or Ordinary; 2) selected directly by the leader that they will serve; or 3) selected by the Adjutant-General of the reformation. When inside the church, the adjutants have charge of the processionals, habit, vesture, and crowd movement inside the sanctuary. Following the concept of having a structured organization, there are levels or ranks among the Adjutancy, which will be briefly described here. (Not all described are included in the diagram.)

Ranks within the Adjutancy:

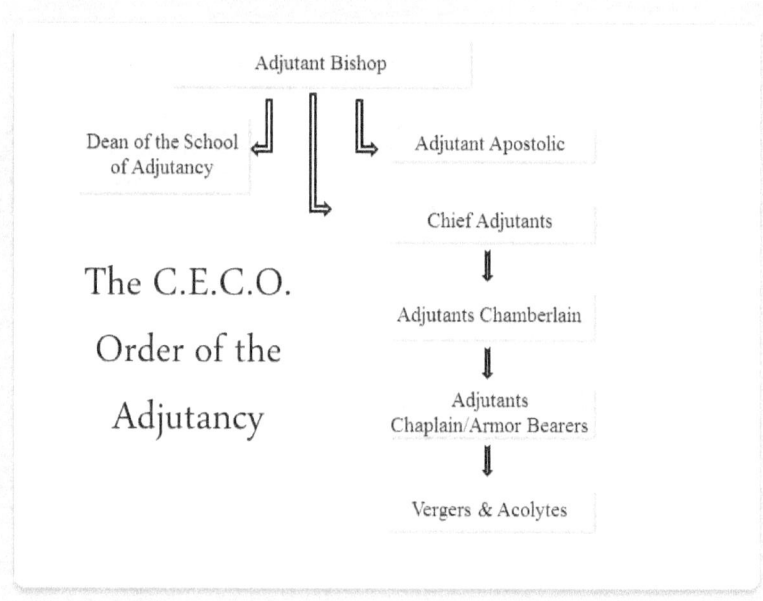

National Adjutancy: (These adjutants serve on a "National" level within the Reformation and are called upon for the management of this servant-ministry. These officers are called to serve at any deliberate gathering of the Fellowship.)

Bishop of Protocol

This prelate, as an advisor to the Primate, is selected by the Presiding Bishop of the Fellowship and approved by the Executive Council. This officer is one who is well versed in Church Ceremonial and has direct oversight of all matters pertaining to protocol and church etiquette, credentials and certifications, altar works, adjutancy and liturgical order in the Fellowship.

The Bishop of Protocol is called upon to establish a uniform standard amongst the churches of the Fellowship in promoting our vision. This individual has oversight of the Adjutancy as a whole, including the establishment of a code of dress, the School of Adjutancy, the enforcement of protocols and other directives as designated by the Presiding Bishop.

As such, all adjutants in the Fellowship, at the national as well as local levels, fall under the supervisory guidance of the Office of Protocol.

First Assistant

The First Assistant to the Bishop of Protocol works as the right hand of the Bishop of Protocol, carrying out all directives and orders set forth from this Office. It is also the responsibility of the First Assistant to assist the Bishop of Protocol through the Dean of our School, in the mentoring and shaping of adjutants. The First Assistant serves as liaison between the Dean, and the Directors of Protocol, Altar Works and Credentialing and Certifications within the Office of Protocol.

Adjutant-Apostolic

The Adjutant-Apostolic directly serves the Presiding Bishop on a daily basis and at all gatherings of the Fellowship. This rank is generally a mark of distinction for the one who directly assists the Presiding Bishop of the Fellowship and one which holds no direct authority to set or change policy within the Fellowship.

Dean of the School of Adjutancy

CECO's Dean of the School of Adjutancy reports directly to the Adjutant-General and serves at the national level of the Fellowship. This officer is a well-rounded servant that has successfully and faithfully served as Adjutant-Chaplain, Adjutant-Chamberlain and Chief Adjutant of a local assembly within the Fellowship (not necessarily concurrently). This officer of the Adjutancy is largely a curriculum developer and policy writer for the School and has responsibilities as teacher and mentor of adjutants of the Fellowship.

In light of these things, it should be understood that this officer is not within the direct "chain of command" or line of succession as it pertains to the hierarchy for CECO's Order of the Adjutancy. This is due to the need for this officer to maintain focus on the School of Adjutancy and address items which may not impact the Fellowship on a national level. This line of separation between the School and the Fellowship is necessary so that aspiring adjutants and servants outside of the Fellowship can participate in and benefit from training and certification from the School, without being directly affiliated with CECO. In short, one does not need be directly associated with CECO as a member to receive the benefit of the training we produce at its School.

It is the responsibility of the Dean to, as aforementioned, develop curriculum for gatherings of the Fellowship. This includes individual, local and regional training sessions and of course the curriculum of the School of Adjutancy. The Dean works with the Adjutant-General to transpose the Spirit of Adjutancy onto paper and convey that through the training sessions to the adjutants and servants of the Fellowship.

Local Adjutancy (the local adjutant serves on a level which is subordinate to the national. These adjutants have the daily care of the Bishops of Dioceses and directly represent the local assembly in their area.)

NOTE:
Not all local assemblies within CECO will have need of each of these adjutants. Most bishops/pastors at the local level will only require the services of one adjutant and this adjutant is designated as Adjutant-Chamberlain to that subordinate bishop.

Chief Adjutant

This adjutant is to work closely with the administrative staff of the bishop to be apprised of all ministerial events in order to schedule those adjutants who will ensure the proper care of the bishop. In the instances where an Ordinary has need of more than one adjutant, it is the Chief who is ultimately responsible for the vesting, care of and service to the bishop as well as his insignia and properties although he may appoint others to the direct service. This adjutant has the understanding, loyalty and capacity to serve as either Chamberlain or Chaplain in their absence.

The Chief Adjutant of the local assembly or region is responsible for ensuring all directives are received and understood from the national level and disseminated to the local church he serves. It is further the responsibility for the Chief Adjutant to see to the development and training of the adjutants under his charge, under the direction of the Adjutant-General. Lastly, we should mention that this servant is one who has served successfully (and may continue to serve) as Adjutant-Chamberlain to an Auxiliary, Coadjutor or Ordinary Bishop.

Adjutant-Chamberlain

This office is the local version of the Adjutant-Apostolic in that they are responsible for directly serving the subordinate (Coadjutor) bishop. The Adjutant-Chamberlain personally assists in the proper vesting of the Prelature and is usually adjutant to the Bishops of Dioceses or those of the local church. This adjutant is the one in the local assembly who handles and maintains the bishop's vestments and insignia and it is because they are familiar with their bishop and his/her vestments, it is expected that they be utilized during vesting within the gatherings of the Fellowship. This adjutant is also responsible for selecting the appropriate vesture based on the occasion and the dress code disseminated by the Chief Adjutant. While the Chief Adjutant of a local assembly may have oversight of the adjutants under his charge, the Adjutant-Chamberlain will serve the local prelate most closely. It should be noted that one may serve successfully as both Chief Adjutant and Adjutant-Chamberlain in their local church.

Adjutant-Chaplain

This person works closely with the bishop's Episcopal administrator to stay apprised of the bishop's itinerary to make necessary arrangements for travel and accommodation. The non-ordained and/or non-administrative version of this position is an Armor-Bearer. There could be one Adjutant-Chamberlain with multiple Adjutant-Chaplains or Armor-Bearers working with them, or a bishop could appoint multiple Adjutant-Chamberlains and they could all rotate their service. This is of course, solely dependent upon the needs and desires of that particular prelate. The Adjutant-Chaplain serves as driver and clerk to his prelate.

Again, we point out that some prelates may only require the use of one adjutant this is perfectly acceptable. In this regard, said adjutant will serve as chaplain and chamberlain to his prelate and his work will envelop the duties of both.

Vergers & Acolytes

These persons are appointed by Bishops of the Dioceses (Ordinaries) and may be selected by the Chief Adjutant at any given ceremony, as need arises in the local church. They serve as Processional Cross Bearer, Processional Banner Bearers, Bible Bearer and candle lighters. These offices are designated for our youth with the intent that as they serve, these persons are being groomed for more demanding roles within the Adjutancy. As Proverbs 22:6 declares, "Train up a child…" With this appointment as an acolyte or verger, a spirit of servant-hood and humility is cultivated within our young persons as we rear our successors to this great and ongoing work.

Honoring the Episcopacy

As you serve your bishop and throughout this Servant-Ministry, you will encounter a great many people who may not know what a bishop is, or what the office entails. Some will not know how to greet your bishop and because of their ignorance of Episcopal matters, they will not know how to properly honor the prelate you serve. One of the responsibilities of the adjutant is to be the voice of the bishop in matters that he should not speak to lest he seem self-serving.[3] Oft times, all that is necessary is a humble reminder that speaks to the infraction and the problem will be quickly resolved. The correction that is given in humility and love is most often greeted with understanding and action.

The adjutant is perpetually (and simultaneously) engaged in three activities: serving, learning and teaching. Serving in that the Adjuancy is not a 9-5 gig to be picked-up and put-down on a whim. This Servant-Ministry is a lifetime of service and not just a job at which anyone 'off the street' can succeed. At any time, the adjutant can be called upon by his prelate to whatever end necessary. The adjutant needs to prepare themselves as well as their family for this level of service. Preparing oneself obviously entails much prayer, humility, patience, strength in the Spirit, study of the Word, study of ecclesiastical texts and so on. Preparing ones family can be a more difficult task as one MUST engage their family in the service of which they are a part. The adjutant who has not seen to the needs of his family is misrepresenting his prelate. This looks as if the prelate has no thought for his adjutant's family at all which should not be the case. If the adjutant sees to the needs of his family, then he can be free to fully engage in this Servant-Ministry. This encompasses everything from cutting the grass and taking out the trash before a long weekend of service, to balancing time spent with one's family so they do not feel overwhelmed or offset by your work in the church, to covering your family spiritually and teaching biblical principles as ordained in the word of God.

The adjutant is always learning, not only through study of God's word and Godly curriculum but in observing as well. The adjutant is to ALWAYS watch his leader and take the queue from him. Eventually, through relationship, time spent together in ministry and the connection of the Spirit, the adjutant will begin to sound and make decisions like his bishop. This is not to say that it is the aim of the Episcopacy to create clones or robots among those that serve in the Adjutancy. The adjutant carries the spirit of his leader and in his service he cannot help but to emulate his prelate, this is a desired trait that takes years to develop so one should not expect to spiritually resemble one's leader so soon after assignment. It should be the intent of all of us to reproduce after our kind.

The adjutant is always teaching by way of his actions. We will briefly explore the aspect of teaching through example as it pertains to honoring your prelate and sanctifying him in the eyes of the people. As aforementioned, most people (believers as well) do not know very much as it pertains to the Episcopacy. They will learn through YOUR example. What it means to sanctify your prelate in the eyes of the people directly relates to how you physically serve. Represent your prelate well and show proper deference to his Office, (not for outward show, but to be an ensample to the flock), and he will be honored by the people in kind. This is not to suggest that you, as adjutant, are to appear cultish in your service or set your prelate on a pedestal. This simply means to serve with honor, humility and great care remaining always attentive yet not overbearing in service to your officer.

Reflections

- Are you in a position to be trustworthy enough to cover your leaders' weakness?
- Due to the vast nature of the adjutancy, it is imperative that you seek clarification and gain understanding from your leader regarding your function as an adjutant or armor bearer.

Chapter IV

Episcopal Orders

There are six orders of Prelature in the Church of Jesus Christ. This hierarchy allows the decentralization of authority and for different territories of the Church to be governed with the appropriate amount of attention and care. Once a prelate is assigned to an Order amongst the Prelature, this assignment is not for life and further appointment is subject to the needs of the Fellowship.

Five of the Orders of Prelature are Episcopal, meaning consecrated bishops alone hold these offices, and one is potentiary.[1] This potentiary office is so called owing to the fact that this individual is a Overseer with the potential to be raised to the Bishopric. It is practiced in this Fellowship that when the need arises, prelates who desire the office of a bishop are considered from the ranks of the Overseers.

Here, we will outline the six Orders of Prelature and offer a brief description as to the scope of each.

The Order of Prelature is as follows:
 a) Presiding Bishop (primate)
 b) Ordinary (diocesan or territorial bishops)
 c) Coadjutor
 d) Auxiliary
 e) Suffragan
 f) Overseer

4a. The **Presiding Prelate** is perhaps the most celebrated and recognized Episcopal Order in the Church. This is the Chief Consecrator and Primate amongst his fellow episcopates and all others fall under his leadership and spiritual guidance within the Fellowship. This bishop is elected from among the bishops of the Fellowship in a closed session termed Conclave.

Conclave is a private and closed-door session of the prelates of the Fellowship. During conclave, matters can span the discussion of serious disciplinary infractions and the deciding of outcomes; this where spiritual battle plans are drawn and where the direction of the Fellowship is decided among the most senior leadership. It is during conclave, when the Fellowship's Cathedra is empty, that a new Presiding Bishop is elected by the Executive Council. It is also during these sessions that other prelates and officers within the Fellowship are elected to office.

The Presiding Bishop shall always serve as the Chief Consecrator and Ordainer for all persons elevated to the Bishopric within the Church.[2] When the time arises for such a consecration to take place, there must be at least two other consecrated bishops present as Co-Consecrators who will stand with him. Never must anyone who is not a consecrated bishop operate in this capacity for the consecration of a bishop. Should anyone be raised any other way, they will not be recognized as a properly raised bishop and as such, must seek the proper way with patience and much grace.

4b. The **Ordinary** or Diocesan bishop generally exercises authority in and has oversight of an Apostolic province or district within the Fellowship. However, there are different classes of Ordinaries, those who exercise territorial jurisdiction, and those who do not. Therefore, Ordinary jurisdiction can be personal or territorial. Concerning personal jurisdiction, all prelates exercise this scope of authority. They hold the authority to legislate, adjudicate and generally govern a body of people, thus their jurisdiction is to individuals, not to a locus.

Concerning Ordinaries who exercise territorial jurisdiction, all churches within an assigned territory are governed by their territorial or Ordinary Bishop. This setup allows for the proper flow of authority, orders and directives following the Apostolic Order of the Fellowship.

When there is a candidate for ordination within a local church, the senior pastor presents this candidate to the Ordinary for consideration. Following the recommendation of the senior pastor, the testimony of his clerical staff, and ultimately the leading of the Holy Spirit, it is this prelate who has the authority to administer Holy Orders, by the anointing with oil and laying on of hands, to ordain elders and deacons in local churches. This authority does not rest within the senior pastor (unless he himself is a consecrated bishop). Bishops ordain elders, with the assistance of overseers or other ordained elders and the elders become the property of the whole Church. Only bishops ordain deacons because they are the "property" of the bishop, on assignment to the local churches.[3]

The Ordinary is selected by the Presiding Bishop and the appointment is approved by the Executive Council of this Fellowship. This officer speaks for the pastors in his territory and represents the churches under his charge at gatherings of the Fellowship and at conclave. In this way, the Ordinary is the voice of the diocese and handles all disciplinary matters of a more serious nature. Said disciplinary matters are brought to the territorial prelate via the senior pastors of that province according to the Fellowship's Code of Canon.

4c. The **Coadjutor** serves as the chief assistant to an Ordinary in the territory. This prelate has immediate right to succession within the territory, yet he exercises limited authority while the Ordinary is in office. Mainly, the Coadjutor serves as the executor of the Ordinary's directives and is appointed to those Sees impeded from the performance of their Episcopal duties.[4] A Coadjutor may also be appointed to an Ordinary with a territory of such scope that they require additional governance. Due to the nature of their functionality, it is not necessary that all territories make use of a Coadjutor. The Coadjutor governs in the stead of the Ordinary to carry out all Episcopal duties.

During meetings of the diocese, weddings, funerals, ordinations or celebrations of the like, the Coadjutor performs these functions in the absence of the Ordinary. The Coadjutor does not make policy for the diocese, he carries out the policy set forth by the Ordinary. Further, the Coadjutor can function as a buffer or go-between for the Ordinary to address matters in his stead.

4d. The **Auxiliary** bishop is an administrative role at the National or Diocesan level. This prelate executes his office without diocesan oversight and as such, this prelate has no right to succession. At the publication of this manual, the Executive Secretary of CECO is an Auxiliary bishop. This function does not diminish the Episcopal authority of this individual; it simply provides a focus and directs the intent of this prelates' work within the Fellowship.

If this officer serves on the National level, the Presiding Bishop of the Fellowship makes this appointment. If the office is on the diocesan level, then the Ordinary of that particular diocese may appoint this individual to office.

4e. The **Suffragan** bishop is the fifth order of Prelature. This bishop is a member of the Presiding Bishop or Ordinary's Cabinet, without right of succession.[5] This office is mainly administrative in nature. Districts within a large province or Apostolic See may be assigned to this bishop for administrative governance. As with the coadjutor, not all territories will make use of a suffragan bishop.

4f. The sixth order of Prelature is the **Overseer**. A major difference in this office as compared to the preceding five is that the Overseer is appointed by the Presiding Prelate, as opposed to being consecrated for service. Should the need arise within the Fellowship, officers from these ranks shall be considered for elevation to the Bishopric. The sixth order of prelature is often termed "potentiary" for this cause; these have the potential to be one day raised as bishops.[6]

The Overseer serves as the right hand of the Senior Bishop (Presiding Prelate, Coadjutor), as an assistant in the managing of districts within a diocese. This officer also may serve as an executive board member within said territory. Due to their lack of Episcopal Consecration, it is generally held that these Prelates do not attend conclave unless expressly invited by the Presiding Prelate of the Fellowship. Overseers do not have authority or jurisdiction in and of themselves and it is by the nature of their Apostolic Appointment that they may execute their office.[7] Overseers may assist in the ordination of elders and deacons only, as these prelates are not consecrated themselves, they may not participate as concelebrants at any Episcopal consecration.

Chapter V

Episcopal Insignia

When we see a badge, no matter in what country, we associate that symbolic imagery with law and order, and institutions that enforce the law. When we see a stethoscope and a white lab coat, we relate those items to practitioners in the medical field and their commitment to saving lives. Much like these professional positions and institutions, there are Episcopal Insignia, which represent timeless traditions of the universal Church. The term Episcopal insignia is symbolic of one's Episcopal office and or apostolic see.

A. The Episcopal Ring

The Episcopal ring is perhaps the most recognized article of insignia pertaining to prelatial dignity. When worn, the ring is to adorn the fourth finger of the wearer's right hand. This finger is known as the "ring finger", relating to the wedding band worn similarly on the left hand of those joined in holy matrimony. This is significant because the Episcopal ring symbolizes the spiritual marriage of the bishop to the Church and his dedication to such. It is commonly held that when the Episcopal ring is worn, no other ring is to be worn on either hand, save the wedding band. The Episcopal ring is also symbolic of son-ship as illustrated when the prodigal son returned to his father it was instructed that the servants "put a ring on his hand, and shoes on his feet" (Luke 15:22).

There are two Episcopal rings in use today, the gemmed, which is most commonly seen, and the ordinary, which bears the arms of the prelate. The gemmed ring may vary in size and shape; it may bear diamonds or be unadorned. With these freedoms however, there are some constants in the design of the gemmed ring. Episcopal rings will bear an amethyst (a stone reserved for Bishops) and will be gold in color. These are traditions that have been passed down through the centuries and are easily recognized and accepted abroad.

The ordinary Episcopal ring bears the arms of the prelate and was used generally for sealing documents and to provide authenticity. The use of wax seals have fallen away some over time but continues to be used in the authenticating of Church documents, not necessarily for the purpose of sealing secrets. This type of ring is not as widely seen as the gemmed and most prelates make the use of a stand-alone seal to endorse official documents.

Reverencing the Episcopal Ring

The reverencing of the Episcopal ring refers to kissing the ring of a prelate. This display of respect is mostly in the Eastern nations as the culture of we in the West are lead to view this type of reverence as cultish and quite outdated. It seems that even some prelates view this action toward themselves in that the faithful are honoring them personally, yet this should not be the case. When one chooses to kiss the ring of a prelate, they are in fact honoring Christ whom the bishop represents. As it concerns formal protocol, everyone must genuflect (gentlemen bow, ladies curtsy) before kissing the ring of a prelate to show proper deference to the office and representative of Christ. When exposed to this type of symbolic reverence, prelates are expected to accept the gesture with much grace lest they be seen as self-serving or the like. Should our bishop be approached and asked if one may kiss the ring, we as adjutants are to be especially watchful. At the risk of appearing paranoid, we are to be ever watchful when the bishop is in our care, especially of those who desire to be close to his personage as everyone's intentions are not always holy.

B.   The Crozier

The Crozier, more commonly referred to as the pastoral staff, carried by bishops is symbolic of their role in the lives of the church as shepherd and watchman of our souls. This symbolism speaks to the pastoral authority of bishops as they lead much after the fashion of Moses leading the children of Israel.

There are many designs, materials, shapes and sizes of croziers accepted today, they might be jeweled, gold, wood or quite plain. With all these differences, there remain a few things constant throughout. There are three distinct parts of a crozier, the crook, the staff, and the pediment or pointed bottom shaft. All prelates are authorized the use of the crozier yet as a rule, only those exercising jurisdiction do so.

Protocol:

- When carried in procession, the bishop carries the staff in his left hand, in step with either foot strike (not hovering above the ground) and with the crook always facing forward as he administers jurisdiction over the territory.
- When a crozier bearer is used in procession the bearer (usually the bishop's adjutant) either carries the crozier in his right hand and always slightly above the ground or in both hands with the staff across his chest, allowing the crook to fall over his right shoulder. When carrying the crozier, the adjutant always carries it with the crook facing to the rear unless it is held stationary beside the bishop in which case the crook is facing forward.

C.   The Pectoral Cross

Unlike the crozier, the pectoral cross is not a symbol of jurisdiction but one of dignity. The significance of the pectoral cross is that it is symbolic of the cross that Christ carried to and was hung from at Golgotha. The bearer of the pectoral cross is stating that as Christ died for us, we live for him and keep him in our hearts. Hence, the wearer keeps the pectoral cross in the left breast pocket (nearest the heart) while in civic or clerical attire.

The pectoral cross of prelates is to be gold and of Latin design, meaning that the upper portion and the arms must be of equal length while the lower remains longer. There are two distinctions between the pectoral crosses of prelates. There is the ordinary which is to be worn during daily offices and when the prelate is dressed in civic attire, and there is the pontifical cross. The pontifical cross is traditionally more ornate than the ordinary cross and is worn during High-Church services when the prelate is vested in choir. We do not hold a distinction between crosses of prelates in CECO in their occasion for wear, but we do distinguish in the cord or chain to which it is affixed.

All bishops of the Fellowship are to wear their gold pectoral cross suspended from a gold chain of at least 40 inches in length. The pectoral cross is expected to be worn at all times during the bishop's public ministry, even when a basic suit and tie is worn.

When in Choir Dress, bishops of the Fellowship will don the green and gold cord with their pectoral cross. With the exception of the presiding prelate, this is the only other cord from which a bishop's cross may be suspended. The presiding prelate of the Fellowship dons the *red and gold pectoral cross cord for ceremonies and occasions where choir dress is required.

D.   A Few Words on Heraldry

As servants of the prelature, we will see and sometimes compose missives, official correspondence and documents on the behalf of our bishop. Many times, affixed to said official communiques will be what we refer to as the "seal of the bishop". This seal is composed of that particular bishop's coat-of-arms, a unique and personal representation of the office and personage of the episcopate to whom it belongs. The bishop's seal or personal coat-of-arms is a very visual representation of the bishop which speaks to the authenticity of the document to which it is affixed. By placing one's seal onto a document, it is as if the prelate himself were standing before the reader proclaiming: "I certify this document to be valid and true, furthermore I approve its contents by affixing my name and seal thereupon." This is why members of the adjutancy must guard the seal and images of the episcopacy, to protect the seal is to protect the name of your bishop.

The traditional creation of a coat-of-arms is no haphazard occurrence, but a thoughtful process adhering to regulations and principles. This art form is what is known as Heraldry, and for our purposes, Ecclesiastical Heraldry. Heraldry is simply defined as the practice of devising, blazoning, and granting armorial insignia and of tracing and recording genealogies.[1] Heraldry is both an art and science. As such, let us state that the topic of heraldry is such a vast and involved subject matter that to attempt to capture its entirety in the few short lines provided by this manuscript would be a grave injustice. In light of this, this section will barely brush the "tip of the iceberg" in touching on this topic.

Many may be aware that heraldry as we know it today has its origins in the identification of European warriors. Fully clad in mail and armor, these warriors would apply an achievement of arms upon their shield (escutcheon) and to their banners to identify them upon the field of battle and at tournaments. The term "coat-of-arms" is derived from the fact that these warriors and knights would have their arms embroidered on the coat, which they wore over their armor.

Soon thereafter, armorial bearings were being painted on personal belongings, livery†, carriages, tent canopies, doors of estates and so on. It was only a matter of time before the Church adopted the practice in the form of personal seals. Let us point out that the shield is the ordinary vehicle of the coat of arms. The shield, being a weapon, of course brings with it images of war and violence. Because of this symbolism, many ecclesiastics have substituted the shield for the oval cartouche, thus producing a less combative representation of the clerical office.

In the Western Church today, we see many shapes, sizes forms colors and displays of episcopal arms, yet for the purposes of simplicity and brevity we will describe some common symbols widely accepted as traditional regarding ecclesiastical heraldry. Should a prelate or servant show interest in the subject, we strongly recommend further study by works from a recognized authority such as Archbishop Bruno B. Heim.

The *Galero* is a Roman hat worn by ecclesiastics for over a thousand years as first bestowed to a cardinal in the color red, by Pope Innocent IV at the First Council of Lyons (A.D. 1245).[2] The galero displayed by prelates is to be green in color bearing twelve tassels or *fiocchi*, as six on either side of the shield consisting rows of one, two and three.

Beneath the *galero* is the shield upon which are placed symbols (charges) determined by the bearer. There are many ways to divide the

---

† livery - the distinctive clothing or badge formerly worn by the retainers of a person of rank.[3]

shield and display charges, all at the design of the armiger, within heraldic guidelines. If a Processional Cross is displayed in the achievement of arms, it is to be placed centered, behind the shield with its base visible beneath the shield.

Often times we will see the crozier and mitre displayed atop the shield. These items are also to be displayed behind the shield with the crozier always on the right (dexter). Beneath the shield, some will make use of a scroll bearing the name of the armiger and or his motto.

Let us briefly point out that heraldry has its own language as seen by our use of certain terms in the previous paragraphs. In example, left and right are instead dexter and sinister. Colors are tinctures, which are divided into four main categories: colors, metals, furs and stains. There are ordinaries, sub-ordinaries, lines of partition, marks of cadence, supporters, crests and the list of difference goes on. In order to describe, or *blazon*, a coat of arms a herald uses these specific terms in a prescribed sequence according to heraldic law. To state anything further on the matter would be to delve into the depths of said law and speak to specifics, which is not our aim in this volume.

As previously stated, the art of heraldry is a subject worthy of independent study, yet one not need be an accomplished heraldist in order to produce a proper achievement of arms. In order to verify the originality of an achievement, one is encouraged to contact their country or regions heraldic registry. This is encouraged for peace of mind and authenticity but not required.

Chapter VI

Ecclesiastical Vestments

There are two methods in the study of Church Vestments, the ritualistic method and the antiquarian. The ritualistic method holds and seeks to prove, that the vestments of the Christian Church are fashioned upon the vestments of the Old Testament priesthood originating with with Exodus 28:4. The description of these garments given by God to Moses implies an "indirect divine appointment for the Christian vestments"[1]; this is greatly the basis of the claim for authenticity of the ritualistic method of study.

The antiquarian method is a "process of gaining knowledge of the vestments of the Church by a study of archaeology and a comparison of the works of authors and artists of successive periods."[2] The graphic imagery from catacombs, mosaics of the early church and mortuary figures of those on ancient tombs provide the most material for study of this method. The experts of this method maintain that the vestments evolved from the ordinary costume of a Roman citizen of the first or second century.

Neither of these schools of thought is absolutely correct, as elements of both hold true. The majority of probability favors the antiquarian method, which, however, does not take into account certain changes in textures and numbers of vestments while the Church was in her infancy.

In the ninth century and on through the Middle Ages, we see information concerning Vestments begins to be quite specific. Before this time, Christian literature and art had been scarce, first due to the persecution of the Church then by wars and upheaval. Further, the span between the ninth and eleventh centuries sees a doubling in the number of vestments recognized by the Church.

Herein is a brief description of the vestments authorized for wear by the Fellowship, Christians Equipping Christians for Outreach. It is our endeavor to share how we within CECO view these garments and put them to use in the service of God.

As a reformation, CECO makes use of garments from both the Roman Catholic and Anglican traditions. These garments are largely recognized and synonymous with the universal Church so as to speak to our brotherhood with other religious bodies.

Cassock
- pronounced: (ka-sek)

The Roman cassock as we have come to recognize it today is of early fifth-century French origins. Despite this, it was not until the twelfth and thirteenth centuries that the cassock became solely identified with the Church. As the Renaissance approached, the simple cloak lined with animal skin or fur transformed and became "Romanized" as its roughness faded away to be replaced with color and rich materials.[3] The cassock is normally worn a colorless black with no embellishments or piping variations. As a symbol of the servant, the cassock is worn by ministers, elders and all prelates of the Fellowship. This simple garment traditionally has 33 buttons down the front from Roman collar to hem in remembrance of the life of Christ. When worn, the cassock should be long enough to cover the ankles of the wearer yet it should not drag the floor.

The prelature generally make use of two different styles of cassock: the choir cassock and the house cassock (also called the ordinary cassock). The house cassock follows the design of all Roman cassocks with its full-cut, loose fit and bell shape. This cassock is all black with piping along the seams in the color of the wearer's office (usually fuchsia or scarlet). The house cassock is worn by prelates for preaching occasions and when going about the daily offices if so desired. Generally, the house cassock is not to be worn outside of the See and is reserved for use during private ceremonies and in the local church. In CECO, consecrated prelates alone are afforded the option to wear the house cassock.

The choir cassock is so named because it is worn by prelates in choir, that is, in the portion of the church located between the congregational seating area (the Nave) and the area around the altar (the Chancel). These terms are borrowed from Gothic architecture when immense cathedrals were being built in major European cities.

The choir cassock may also be worn at public ceremonies and special events on church property if so desired by the prelate. Today's choir cassock is red-purple or fuchsia in color and otherwise follows the design of the ordinary/house cassock. The choir cassock is retained for use at the most solemn liturgical occasions where choir dress is required.[4] When in traditional choir dress, the choir cassock will always be worn under the rochet as opposed to the all-black or house cassock.

The use of ordinary cassock is not as prevalent as the "higher" garments used for celebrations, yet it remains a garment of the prelate to be worn at his discretion.

Protocol:

- The cassock worn by members of this Fellowship will be of the Roman style bearing buttons down the front. Said buttons will be either working or faux concealing a simple snap and will be no more than 33 or no less than 10 in number.
- In CECO, the cassock is reserved for wear by members of the clergy; this includes licensed and ordained Ministers, Deacons, Elders, Pastors, Overseers, Apostles and Bishops.
- When properly worn, the cassock will be long enough to cover the ankles. The only clergy authorized the use of a colored cassock during gatherings of the Fellowship are Prelates. No one is authorized the use of a white cassock save the Presiding Prelate in the absence of the Metropolitan. Prelates may wear CECO's colors or a cassock denoting their office commensurate with the occasion where precise uniformity is not required. All others will wear the black colorless cassock.

Cincture

- pronounced: (sink-cher)

Because of the loose fit of the cassock, the cincture or fascia was implemented to hold the garment in place above the waist. Later, use of the garment was retained as a symbol of one's commitment to a life of servant hood. The symbolism is derived from the occasion wherein Christ girded himself with a towel about the waist and washed his disciples' feet. (John 13:5) Herein, the clergy, especially adjutants, take our cue as being servants of all.

The standard cincture worn by the clergy of CECO will be of the band variation and shall be 4-6 inches in width, having both ends terminate in fringe. The black cincture is the only cincture authorized for wear by non-consecrated clergy of CECO. During gatherings of the Fellowship, Prelates of CECO will be directed as to the attire for wear dependent upon the occasion, this will include the Roman Purple (choir), chianti (CECO colors), scarlet, black or black trimmed in scarlet piping (to accompany the House cassock). Again, the attire will largely be dictated by the nature of the gathering, be it Holy Convocation, conclave or a consecration. It is of course up to the Adjutancy to communicate and be aware of the occasion and ensure their prelates are appropriately vested.

It should be known that the Presiding Prelate of this Fellowship reserves the right of the use of the white cincture to match his cassock. The Metropolitan of CECO is also authorized the use of the white cincture. When properly worn, the cincture flaps will fall to the left of the wearer, but not so far as to rest past the left hip. The two hanging portions of the cincture will overlap in such a way, that the flap closest the wearer will hang lower than the forward facing flap, allowing for visibility of both fringed edges of the garment.

While the intent of the cincture is to hold in place and gather the otherwise loose fitting cassock and alb, it is not a belt and as such, it should not be worn so. The proper placement of the cincture shall be above the wearer's normal waistline, generally in line with the navel.

Protocol:

- Only those ordained will utilize the cincture when in cassock and the cincture shall be 4-6 inches in width.
- Prelates alone are authorized the use of colored cinctures with tasseled ends. All others shall be black and end in fringe.
- When in Choir Dress, Prelates of the Fellowship shall wear the Fuchsia or "Bishop's Cincture".

Surplice
- pronounced (ser-ples)

The surplice is perhaps the most recognizable of liturgical garments and came into general use in the Church by the eighth century. This garment has been in continual use for over one thousand years and is one of the oldest in use by the Church today. Like the rochet, the surplice has roots in the alb and is an all-white garment worn only over cassock. The garment is symbolic of purity and holiness, which the minister adorns in his service to the Lord. The surplice is required for wear when the pastor is in choir dress.

The standard surplice worn in CECO is of the Roman design; that is, having an unadorned (plain) front and square yoke. The lace-trimmed surplice is authorized for wear by senior pastors of the churches of the Fellowship. The surplice authorized for wear during gatherings of the Fellowship shall bear a square yoke with its hem reaching the knees of the wearer

Protocol:

- All surplices in the Fellowship will be knee length.
- Only Adjutants who are ordained Elders and Senior Pastors of the Fellowship will make use of the surplice.
- All surplices worn will bear the square yoke, Roman for adjutants, lace trimmed for Senior Pastors when in Choir Dress.

Rochet

- pronounced: (rah-chet or ro-shaý)

The rochet as we recognize it today was developed in the fourteenth century. The garment takes its name from Old French, yet its origins are from the Latin *rochettus*. The rochet is not a liturgical garment yet it is always worn when the prelate is vested in choir. This garment symbolizes purity and the Priesthood that was given to Aaron and his sons. When the priests entered in to the Most Holy place, they were covered with the garments "for glory and for beauty" so as to reflect the image and purity of God.

The rochet should never be confused with the surplice nor should they be viewed as interchangeable garments. The rochet is a garment reserved for use by the prelates of CECO to include our Overseers as the sixth order of prelature. The traditional rochet is the only style that shall be worn by prelates of the Fellowship. This garment is greatly distinguished by its sleeves, which are closed by detachable wristbands and pleated cuffs. Said cuffs can be procured in colors to match the chimere denoting the rank of the prelate. (CECO's Overseers wear black cuffs only, other prelates will wear fuchsia or scarlet as designated by their Episcopal office.)

The rochet may be worn uncovered, that is, without chimere or any other garment over it. The uncovered rochet is a sign of Ordinary Jurisdiction.[5]

Protocol:

- The colored bands on the cuffs of the rochet will always match the chimere (when worn).
- CECO's Overseers will wear black wristbands only.

Chimere

- pronounced: (sha-mir)

The chimere is regarded as a vestment of jurisdiction; hence the Prelates of the Church who exercise jurisdiction over an Apostolic See or territories wear it. The term jurisdiction further refers to one having authority over a given territory or the right to exercise authority and govern. The traditional chimere has its origins in the Church of England and is historically an Anglican garment. Regardless as to its origin, this Fellowship makes use of the chimere when the prelate is vested in choir. This is a sleeveless cloak, which is open down the front, and fastened by a simple rope looped over a button across the chest.

Resembling an academic gown without sleeves, this garment is worn black by overseers and church purple, chianti or scarlet by episcopates within the Fellowship, as designated by the occasion and station of the prelate.

(Note: Regarding the colors of Ecclesiastical and Clerical attire, at no time should one's attire "outrank" in color, that of the Presiding Prelate. If the occasion calls for the Presiding Prelate of the Fellowship to don his civic attire, all prelates, regardless as to episcopal designation are to follow suit. If the Presiding Prelate opts to wear a church-purple chimere, all other episcopates are to wear black in deference to his office as Chief Episcopate. This is not a written "rule" but a simple matter of Episcopal Protocol.)

Protocol:
- Overseers wear the black chimere only, all other prelates may wear a colored chimere (roman purple, chianti or scarlet)
- The Presiding Prelate is the only Episcopate authorized the use of a white chimere in the absence of the Metropolitan.
- When the chimere is worn, the episcopate wears his pectoral cross beneath the rope closure.

Tippet
- pronounced (ti-pet)

The Tippet is described as a, "long black scarf worn over the robe by Anglican clergyman during morning and evening prayer."[6] Generally, this definition is true as this was the original intent of the garment in response to the historical stole. The tippet is a symbol of the "yoked one" and representative of the jurisdiction of the prelate and receipt of the full weight and burden of service.

The garment is a colorless black and hangs down the front of the neck of the wearer with either panel of the garment measuring 50" long. Overseers and those of the prelature are authorized the use of the tippet as they are officers who exercise jurisdiction within the National Fellowship.

It is custom to affix the seal of one's Fellowship to the left panel (from the perspective of the wearer) and the Episcopal Seal on the right for those who enjoy the privilege episcopal consecration. All seals shall be affixed six inches from the lower edge of the garment and shall be separated by three inches one from another if more than one seal is adorned to either panel.

Protocol:

- The tippet will be black in color and bear a length as to measure 50inches of material hanging down each side of the neck.
- The CECO seal will be affixed to the left side of the tippet (as it is worn). The lower edge of the patch will be six inches from the lower edge of the tippet.
- The use of an Episcopal crest or coat of arms is authorized to be affixed in like fashion to the right panel (from the perspective of the wearer). This patch will be sewn (or embroidered) six inches from the lower edge of the tippet.
- The CECO Seal and any personal Episcopal Arms are the only authorized embellishments to the tippet.

Zucchetto

- pronounced: (zu-ket-to)

Originally developed to protect the crown of the head exposed by tonsure[‡], the zucchetto or skullcap, has carried on as the Bishop's Prayer Cap and is no longer utilized for its originally intended purpose. Use of the zucchetto is reserved for Consecrated Prelates of the Fellowship; said prayer cap will always be worn whenever there is need to don the biretta

---

[‡] Tonsure – the shaven crown or patch worn by monks and other clerics as a rite of admission to the clerical state.

or mitre (when the prelate is vested in choir dress.) The zucchetto comes in three sizes of small, medium and large.

Common colors of the zucchetto are black, fuchsia, scarlet and white. As with most vestments, the colors of the zucchetto will denote ranks within the prelature, leaving red reserved for the Presiding Prelate and white for the Fellowship's Metropolitan.

Protocol:
- The zucchetto will be removed during Prayers of Invocation, readings or hearings of the Gospels of Jesus Christ, Blessings and during the Consecration of the Host. However, the bishop will not remove the cap during the prayer of Consecration at the ordination of elders and deacons, nor the Consecration of Bishops.
- The white zucchetto is reserved for use by the Primate in the absence of the Metropolitan.
- When worn, the zucchetto will sit upon the crown of the head (slightly to the rear), not directly on the top of the head like a ball cap.

Biretta
- pronounced: (buh-ret-uh)

The biretta is a square ecclesiastical cap worn only over the zucchetto.[7] Historical documents of the Renaissance refer to the biretta as the "scholastic cap," identifying its origin. It was not until 1527 that the biretta appears as we now recognize it; however, the permitting of its use by priests was not put into place until a hundred years later.

The top of the cap has three horns, which are worn facing to the front, right and rear with the blank space to the left from the perspective of the wearer. The four-horned biretta is a doctoral cap to be used in academic settings by those who have attained doctoral degrees in Theological Studies. As it is not an ecclesiastical cap, the four-horned biretta will not be worn at gatherings of the Fellowship; it is superseded by the three-horned ecclesiastical cap.

Atop the biretta is a tuft or pompon in either the same or a contrasting color of the cap. The biretta is offered in a variety of colors such as black with a black pompon, black with a scarlet pompon and scarlet trim, all fuchsia, all scarlet or all white. Much like the cassock, white is reserved for use by the Chief Consecrator of the Fellowship. Only consecrated bishops of the Fellowship are authorized the use of the biretta in any color variation.

Protocol:

- The biretta will be worn in choir dress, during High-Church services unless the mitre is required. (This includes but is not limited to consecrations and ordinations.)
- The cap should be worn to fit firmly on the forehead, just above the brow. As aforementioned, the hornless peak should always face to the left, from the perspective of the wearer.
- The cap should only be worn when walking in procession (or recession) and never when attending "in choir." (Referring to the physical portion of the church)
- Following the processional, all episcopates should remove the biretta and especially at the Prayer of Invocation.

Sacred Vestments

Chasuble

- pronounced (`cha-ze-bul)

The chasuble, like many garments prescribed for ecclesiastic wear, finds its origins in a more practical use. Derived from a poncho-like cloak, the chasuble was worn by the working class of the Roman Empire for protection from the elements. By the 3rd century, an earlier version of the chasuble, the casula, became limited for use by high-ranking clergy. Later, in the sixth century the garment became a part of bishop's vesture and grew in elaboration.

There are two main styles of chasuble accepted in today's Church, the Gothic and Roman variation. The Gothic style chasuble, which is the most familiar to us, retains the original poncho-like appearance having no armholes yet an opening for the head alone. The garment is conical in shape, tapering down from the neck. If the wearer were to place his arms straight out to the sides, the garment would form a semicircle. The garment is reserved for occasions of administering the Holy Sacrament, a determination that designates it as a "sacred" vestment.

The Roman style chasuble, also known as the 'fiddle back' will not be worn by CECO's prelature. Strangely enough, despite the name, the fiddle shape is actually seen on the front of the garment and the back is square cut. The Roman chasuble reaches about mid-thigh and is usually adorned with a number of patterns and/or shapes.

Due to the nature of the garment being a 'sacred vestment', most chasubles are seen with elaborate embroidery and are rich in quality deserving of the sacred function of which they form a part. This is in direct opposition to a more mundane garment such as a cassock, which is deliberately plain; therein lays a distinction between the sacred and ecclesiastical vestments.

Alb

The origin of the alb is unable to be pinpointed and remains much a mystery to historians of Ecclesiastical vestments. The first documented mention of the garment was in a letter by Emperor Valerian to Zosimus, procurator of Syria (A.D. 269-270).[8] The alb is to be an all-white garment and will be worn as a singular garment in this Fellowship, that is, it is not a choir vestment.

The white of the garment signifies the purification of the wearer by the washing of the Blood. The alb will be worn by CECO's adjutants who are either licentiates or those of the Diaconate. This is their foremost garment and will be worn during Holy Convocation and for ceremonial use. The Alb shall fit loosely around the wearer as it is not a form-fitting garment, yet it shall be tied at the waist by a white rope cincture with knotted ends.

Cope

The cope is said to be the second most recognizable of the sacred vestments. Usually elaborate in design and ornament, the cope is a cloak that closes at the breast with a chain or single clasp. The cope also bears a hood, which has fallen to disuse and is now strictly kept on as an ornamental addition. The cope was originally designed for wear over the chasuble until the procession reached the interior of the church. Again, it was a functional garment worn to protect the wearer as well as the chasuble from the elements. Its Latin name is *pluvial*, which means "rain catcher".

Today, seeing as how the garment is no longer needed to protect from the elements and has taken on a strictly sacred role in the vestments of the prelate, the cope should never be worn over the chasuble. Rather, when worn it should be donned over the cassock or rochet (if worn), and always fastened at the neck by a simple clasp.

Mitre

- pronounced (mi-ter)

The mitre is a headdress worn by Episcopates of the Church which came into use by the prelature in the tenth century. The mitre is common for having two flaps of material ending in fringe hanging down the prelate's back. These flaps are called "fanons" and are to be trimmed in the same material of the mitre. Traditional miters have an ornamental band across the bottom called a circulus and a vertical band, called the titulus, extending from the middle of the circulus. These bands are not required to identify an "authentic" mitre as present day custom has given rise to many fashions and variations of the traditional mitre.

There are three types of mitre, the precious (*mitra pretiosa*), semi-precious (*mitre auriphrygiata*), and the simple (*mitra simplex*).[9] These types are mentioned here for the sake of historical knowledge as prelates of this Fellowship are not required to maintain their individual use. The precious mitre is to be fashioned of the finest material and adorned with the most exquisite ornamentation and embroidery. The second mentioned mitre is distinguished only in the level of ornamentation as compared to the first. The simple mitre is just that and bears no ornament. Again, CECO's prelates do not distinguish between the three styles of mitre and may don any mitre of design of their choosing so long as it is commensurate with the vestments of a Bishop of the Church.

Protocol:
- Miters may be worn by consecrated bishops of the Fellowship.
- For gatherings of the Fellowship, the Office of Protocol will determine the headdress of the Prelature.
- The Mitre shall be worn in processional, recessional and during certain portions of a consecration and ordination ceremony.

Pallium

- pronounced (pa-lē-um)

The proper insignia of a Metropolitan Archbishop are the pallium and the Archiepiscopal Cross.[10] The pallium is a white woolen circular band, from which hang two pendants of the same material. These pendants are meant to fall down the middle of the back and the center of the breast. There are six black crosses embroidered on the band, one on each shoulder, one at the neck, one at the back and one on each pendant. This garment is to be worn over the sacred vestments while the archbishop is in his jurisdiction and never in choir dress.

The pallium is a symbol of jurisdiction. Only metropolitan bishops (Archbishops) are entitled to the pallium; no other prelate, no matter how high in rank, is entitled to this jurisdictional vesture. The pallium is the last of the sacred vesture to be donned by the metropolitan.

Civic Attire vs. Clerical Attire

There is a misconception among the clergy as to the proper name for attire worn by those in receipt of Holy Orders. This misconception is that the terms Civic attire and Clerical attire are synonymous and as such, the items making up these individual terms are the same. This simply is not the case.

The only color associated with civic attire is that of a colorless-black, regardless as to the rank of the individual. Civic attire consists of black clerical suit, black shoes, black hosiery, and the black breast front. To accomplish this black breast front some opt to make use of the rabat[§] instead of the black clerical shirt. The rabat is secured by elastic bands at the arms and the waist, which can be adjusted for comfort. This item is universal in nature, meaning all those in receipt of Holy Orders may make use of this item for civic dress.

Civic attire is accepted in the Church Universal and one who wears this attire is recognized by all as a "member of the cloth". Civic attire should be donned for public occasions and gatherings with others outside of the Fellowship so as not to confuse or perhaps offend the uneducated.

Clerical attire is different in that those with Episcopal designation make use of colored shirts to denote their rank within the Episcopal Order. While the elder maintains the black clerical shirt, the General Overseer wears a gray neckband shirt with the suit. Further, the consecrated bishop wears the fuchsia, scarlet, blue-purple or red-purple neckband shirt in conjunction with the black suit. Occasions for the wear of clerical attire are, general services, ceremonies (not ordinations), and celebrations within the church where the Holy Sacrament is not served.

[§] By definition, the rabat is a sleeveless, backless, vest like garment extending to the waist and topped with a roman clerical collar.

Chapter VII

Ecclesiastical Protocol and Etiquette

When asked of protocol, as it pertains to the Adjutancy of the Fellowship, most likely the average churchman will state something to the effect that the Adjutancy governs who marches in what order during a processional. While the order of procession does fall to the Adjutancy to manage, this is neither its sole, nor primary vocation. Knowledge of ecclesiastical protocol is unfortunately limited in the Church, even among some of her leaders. The information offered here is not all-inclusive nor does it seek to encompass the entire scope of the Adjutancy, National or Local. It is the aim of this chapter to cover a portion of our duties as the stewards of order in the Church and to provide a basic knowledge and foundation for service and order.

Protocol is defined as, a code prescribing strict adherence to correct etiquette and precedence.[1] The term Ecclesiastical protocol can be interchanged with church discipline however, for the purposes of this manual we will maintain the former verbiage, which is less abrasive. Etiquette of course, is the conduct or procedure prescribed by authority to be observed in social or official life.[2] From these definitions, we see that Ecclesiastical Protocol and Etiquette speak to the code of order and precedence within the Church and allow for a much-needed standard to be set. Exodus 40 directly speaks to this requirement for order in the Church when the Lord Himself instructs Moses in the setup of the tabernacle.

The scope of protocol under the purview of the Adjutancy spans the governance and protection of official church documents, the managing of processionals and recessionals, and the management of ceremonies just to name a few visible areas of concern. In the local assembly, it falls to the Adjutancy to set things in order and work with the ushers and master of ceremonies for the hour, to ensure the senior pastor has much leisure in the execution of the church service.

7a Processionals and Recessionals

Throughout the Liturgical year there will be times when much ceremony and pageantry will be displayed to honor the occasion. This is not to put on "a show", but to exude the appropriate level of reverence due the ceremony and or occasion. When the Israelites marched from place to place, the Ark of the Covenant led them in procession to their destination. When Jesus entered into Jerusalem riding a colt, the people laid palm branches and their garments in the way; there was a procession with Christ at its head. We continue this standard set forth of our Savior leading us in the form of the processional cross taking the head of every procession. Here it may be important to note that there are differences in processional crosses. Processional crosses utilized by CECO will be of Latin design and will not bear a corpus.

Take note that the cross used at all ceremonies of the church should be different than that used by or carried before prelates of the Church. At a cathedral or similar establishment, a second, perhaps larger and more elaborate cross should be reserved for use by the bishop or visiting prelates. This is to signify the eminence of the bishopric and not necessarily to honor the person who the Lord called to the office. This is an honorific and not a 'rule'. The crucifer shall be vested in alb, cassock or similar vestment according to their ecclesiastical rank, but never in plain clothes. This is to show proper honor to the prelate who heads the procession.

Lastly, as it concerns the processional cross, at times when the metropolitan is presiding or serving as chief celebrant, the archiepiscopal cross shall precede him into the sanctuary. This cross bears a second, smaller transverse bar and is appropriately elaborate in adornment. Much like the second processional cross, this is not an absolute requirement.

There are two types or orders of procession, ascending (junior clergy member to senior) and descending (Prelate to minister) order. The occasion, persons present and amount of persons greatly determine the order of procession. Mostly, the order will be decided by the Chief

Celebrant but there will be occasions where there is no preference and the determination for appropriate order will be left to the Adjutancy.

For the purposes of this manual, we will outline an example of processional in both ascending and descending order during a gathering of the Fellowship of the most grand occasion. Take note, when a procession is appropriate, visiting clergy shall always process together in junior position to clergy of the house. This is to show due reverence to the clergy of the house and allows for proper order.

Ascending Order (junior to senior)

This procession will be utilized during national gatherings of the Fellowship, Celebration of the Eucharist, Ordinations and Consecrations and at High Church Services where the clergy is vested in full choir.

Crucifer bearing 1st Processional Cross
Acolytes
Visiting Deacons
Visiting Ministers
Visiting Elders
Visiting Senior Pastors
Adjutants (ascending according to receipt of Holy Orders)
Deacons
Ministers
Elders
Senior Pastors
Crucifer bearing 2nd Processional Cross
Overseers
General Overseers
Visiting Prelates
Adjutant Bishop
Suffragan Bishops
Auxiliary Bishops
Coadjutor Bishops
Ordinary Bishops
*Adjutant Apostolic
Presiding Prelate

All are to stand upon the entrance of the processional cross, and to remain standing until after the call to worship.

Descending Order (senior to junior)

This procession is known as the Civic Procession and is generally utilized when the clergy are in Civic attire, during a Liturgical wedding or at a gravesite.

Crucifer bearing Processional Cross
Acolytes
Presiding Prelate
[5] Adjutant Apostolic
Ordinary Bishops
Coadjutor Bishops
Auxiliary Bishops
Suffragan Bishops
Adjutant Bishop
Visiting Prelates
General Overseers
Overseers
Senior Pastors
Elders
Ministers
Deacons
Adjutants
Visiting Elders
Visiting Ministers
Visiting Deacons

      It will remain the responsibility of the Adjutancy to ensure everyone is in proper order for processional. This responsibility does not fall to the Adjutant Bishop, but is delegated to and administered by the

---

[5] The Adjutant Apostolic will process with the Presiding Prelate's crosier only if he decides not to carry it in procession. Otherwise the Adjutant Apostolic will process in this position empty handed and handle the crosier as appropriate, following the Primate's entry.

adjutants of the Fellowship, working together to ensure proper order and timeliness. If those to process are not in position when the Presiding Prelates takes his place, they simply will not process. The processional will commence when the Presiding Prelate or chief celebrant takes his place. He will not be made to wait upon anyone.

Recessionals will always be led by the Presiding Prelate (preceded by the processional cross) and follow in descending order.

7b Etiquette and Forms of Address

Formalities in the Western Church unfortunately, are not as prevalent as in the Eastern Church. Many view such formalities as insignificant, unnecessary and even 'over the top'. In light of this growing mindset we are reminded of the words of the Apostle Paul to Timothy, *"Let the elders that rule well be counted worthy of double honour, especially they who labour in the word and doctrine." (1 Tim. 5:17)*

One such formality is the arrangement of seating for a banquet or dinner. The main thing that makes a dinner formal is the protocol associated with the event (this includes the dress and etiquette). You can have a formal dinner in the banquet room of the Ritz Carlton Hotel or in the Fellowship Hall in the basement of your church, the location is not the determining factor but how the dinner is conducted makes all the difference in the world.

When conducting dinners, whether formal or informal, and a guest of honor is attending, it is always good form to arrange for proper seating. Let's face it, everyone wants to sit by the Pastor or homilist at dinner but this is just not possible. In light of this, we have prepared a few diagrams to serve as guides when arranging for seating at dinner for your formal or semi-formal occasions.

Seating at a round table

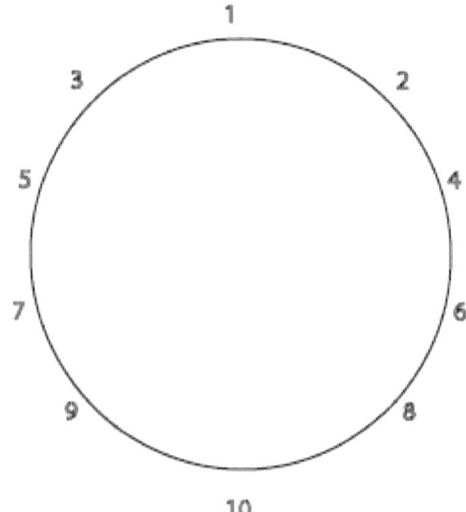

1 – Host
2 – Spouse of Host/Adjutant
3 – Guest of honor/Adjutant
4 – Clergy/Adjutant
5 – Spouse of Guest of Honor
6 – Spouse to #4
7 – Clergy/Adjutant
8 – Senior Layman
9 – Spouse of #7
10 – Senior Prelate/Clergy

Seating at a rectangular table

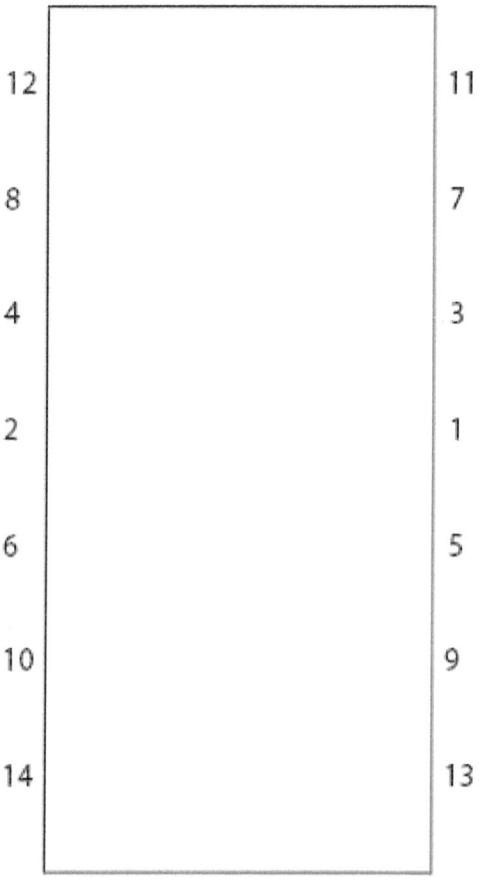

1 – Host
3 – Spouse of host
5 – Senior Prelate/Clergy
7 – Prelate/Clergy
9 – Spouse of #5
11 – Senior Layman
13 – Clergy

2 – Guest of honor
4 – Prelate/Clergy
6 – Spouse of Guest of honor
8 – Spouse of #4
10 – Attendant to Guest of Honor
12 – Guest's Entourage
14 – Guest's Entourage

Seating at a head table

1 – Host
2 – Guest of Honor
3 – Host's Spouse
4 – Guest's Spouse (adjutant)
5 – Master of Ceremonies
6 – Senior Clergy
7 – Clergy
8 – Guest's Entourage
9 – Alternate (clergy or laity)

8
6
4
2
1
3
5
7
9

One should note that these examples are just that, examples. There are a variety of seating arrangements set by occasion and those present. Also, it should be noted that the seating alternates between males and females lastly, the guest and host's spouses are always included. This alternation is of course to include the spouses, as they are, after all, one. As adjutants, we must guard against isolating or even alienating the spouse and children of our leader. At the end of the day our leaders go home and take off his vestments, there he is addressed as "Joe" or "daddy" and we must respect this relationship.

7c Forms of Address

Another way in which we honor our leaders, prelates and the presbytery is in how we address them. As adjutants to our leaders, it is ours to always sanctify them in the eyes of the people. That does not mean that we are to set them upon a pedestal, it speaks to the necessity for us especially to display due reverence and respect to the office our leader holds and the anointing God has entrusted to them. Through time of observance of our example, the people will soon come to reverence our leader in like fashion.

The most commonly used form of verbal address is to use our leader's title. "Good morning Bishop Peat." or "Excuse me Pastor Jones," would be quite sufficient for everyday conversation with the leaders of the Church. One can never go wrong with the use of a title and name along with the usual "sir" or "ma'am" as appropriate. In addition to these forms of proper address, there will be times during ceremonies or formal correspondence where other addresses are required.

The use of formal titles such as "The Right Reverend" and "His Grace" are not a prescribed directive of CECO. These formal titles are used only in high services; in speaking and in our liturgy. The use of these titles is for our uniformity in the Kingdom and hold significance for all of us.

For formal, ceremonial as well as informal forms of address concerning the prelature, presbytery and the diaconate, we offer the following chart as a guide in your conversation as well as correspondence:

The Presiding Prelate

Type of Correspondence	Prescribed Address
Verbal conversation	Bishop or Sir
On an Envelope	Bishop Russell L. Freeman Presiding Bishop of Christians Equipping Christians for Outreach Fellowship
Ceremonial / Formal	His/Your Excellency (Ceremonial) The Most Reverend (formal)
Place Card	Bishop Russell L. Freeman

Bishops

Type of Correspondence	Prescribed Address
Verbal Conversation	Bishop or Sir
On an Envelope	Bishop Herman D. Ware, Jr. (normal)
Ceremonial / Formal	His/Your Grace (Ceremonial) The Right Reverend (formal)
Place Card	Same as Envelope

General Overseers

Type of Correspondence	Prescribed Address
Verbal Conversation	General Overseer or Ma'am
On an Envelope	General Overseer Linda Moss
Ceremonial / Formal	Reverend Ma'am (Ceremonial) The Very Reverend (formal)
Place Card	Same as Envelope

Overseers

Type of Correspondence	Prescribed Address
Verbal Conversation	Overseer
On an Envelope	Overseer Kevin Ware (normal)
Ceremonial / Formal	Reverend Sir (Ceremonial) The Very Reverend (formal)
Place Card	Same as Envelope

Elders or Ordained Clergy

Type of Correspondence	Prescribed Address
Verbal Conversation	Elder
On an Envelope	Elder Alex Plummer
Ceremonial / Formal	Reverend Sir (Ceremonial) The Reverend (formal)
Place Card	Same as Envelope

Deacons

Type of Correspondence	Prescribed Address
Verbal Conversation	Deacon
On an Envelope	Deacon Terrance Luther
Ceremonial / Formal	The Reverend Deacon (Ceremonial) Reverend Deacon Sir (formal)
Place Card	Same as Envelope

Glossary of Terms

GLOSSARY OF TERMS

1. **Eucharist**: communion; spiritual communion with God
2. **Diocese (also referred to as a See)**: administrative division; territorial jurisdiction of a bishop
3. **Liturgy**: a Eucharistic rite; a rite or body of rites prescribed for public worship
4. **Vicar**: one serving as a substitute or agent; an ecclesiastical agent: a member of the Episcopal clergy or laity who has charge of a mission of chapel: a member of the clergy who exercises a broad pastoral responsibility as the representative of a prelate.
5. **Rite**: a prescribed form or manner governing the words or actions for a ceremony; the liturgy of a church or group of churches; a ceremonial act or action
6. **Prelate**: an ecclesiastic (as a bishop or abbot) of superior rank
7. **Primate**: a bishop who has precedence in a province, group of provinces, or a nation; one first in authority or rank: leader
8. **Ecclesiastical**: of or relating to a church especially as an established institution; suitable for use in a church
9. **Sacrament**: a Christian rite (as baptism or the Eucharist) that is believed to have been ordained by Christ that is held to be a means of divine grace or to be a sign or symbol of a spiritual reality; Communion
10. **Cathedra**: the chair or throne of the bishop in his cathedral church from which he presides.
11. **Cathedral**: a church that is the official seat of a diocesan bishop. The cathedral church is the church that is the site of the bishop's cathedra or chair, the sign of his teaching office and pastoral power in the

particular Church. With good reason, then, the cathedral church should be regarded as the center of the liturgical life of the diocese. The cathedral church should be a model for the other churches of the diocese in its conformity to the directives laid down in liturgical documents and books with regard to the arrangement and adornment of churches.

12. **Choir:** an architectural term depicting where the part of the church where the clergy stalls are.
13. **Protocol:** a code prescribing strict adherence to correct etiquette and precedence
14. **Adjutant:** a servant of the church who is well versed in protocol, worship and ecclesiastic ceremony, for the purpose of promoting order in the church and assisting the prelature in all ecclesiastical, ecumenical and Spiritual matters
15. **Holy Orders:** Order is used to signify not only the particular rank or general status of the clergy, but also the outward action by which they are raised to that status, and thus stands for ordination. It also indicates what differentiates laity from clergy or the various ranks of the clergy, and thus means spiritual power. The Sacrament of Order is the sacrament by which grace and spiritual power for the discharge of ecclesiastical offices are conferred.
16. **Primate:** Latin for "first"; a bishop possessing superior authority over several provinces.
17. **Conclave:** a private meeting of episcopates
18. **Code of Canon:** the prescribed regulations set by the Executive Council
19. **High-Church:** favoring especially in Anglican worship the sacerdotal, liturgical, ceremonial, and traditional elements in worship

20. **Choir Dress:** traditional vesture of clerics worn for the administration of the sacraments except when celebrating the Eucharist.
21. **Armiger:** one bearing heraldic arms
22. **English-Purple:** also known as (blue-purple); a variation of the basic color purple as identified in ecclesiastic dress. The term is derived from the Church of England and bears a bluer hue than traditional purple. (violet)
23. **Roman-Purple:** also known as (red-purple or fuschia); a variation of the basic color purple as identified in ecclesiastic dress. This color originates in Roman vestments and is identified as having a redder hue than traditional purple.

APPENDIX

CECO Code of Dress

The vestments worn by CECO's clergy are described in greater detail in Chapter VI of this manual, so we will not belabor the point with redundancy as to descriptions and history. We will however, point out the variances in the Clerical and Liturgical attire amongst those bearing Holy Orders as well as those serving the Adjutancy.

Note: Shoes for women in Civic, Clerical or Liturgical attire/vestments regardless as to standing shall be all black and close-toed. The black suit worn by females may have a skirt or a pants, this is at the discretion of the wearer. Needless to say, should a skirt be worn it shall be of modest length and tailored so as not to bring undue attention to the minister. In all things, we are to maintain that we are a very physical representation of Christ here on earth and we must seek to represent him in all avenues of our life, both public and private. All other attire requirements are synonymous between males and females.

The Adjutancy

As it pertains to Liturgical attire, that is, attire worn during gatherings of the Fellowship, ceremonies, ordinations and the like, the **Adjutant** who has been **licensed** to preach the Gospel or **ordained** to serve as a **deacon** will don the white front wrap Alb. The alb will be of appropriate length covering the ankles of the wearer and shall be plain in design without hood, lace or embroidery. Securing the alb at the front will be a white rope cincture tied appropriately. Over the Alb, the adjutant is authorized the wear of the fuchsia cord with a silver cross affixed. This is to be a standard cross of Latin design, no greater than 3"in height and shall be silver in color.

The Clerical attire for the **adjutant** who has been **ordained** an **Elder** shall be a modest black suit, black hosiery and black shoes. The black neckband shirt with Roman collar is also a part of this attire, said collar shall measure 1 ¼" in height. During gatherings of the Fellowship, adjutants who are Elders will wear the fuchsia cord with silver cross affixed while in clerical and liturgical attire. While in clerical attire, this cross is to be placed in the left breast pocket of either the shirt or the suit jacket at the discretion of the elder.

The Liturgical attire for the **adjutant** who has been **ordained** an **Elder** shall be the black Roman cassock with the black band cincture. Said cassock shall be plain in design with no piping or embroidery. The proper wear of the cassock is that it should be long enough to cover, not merely reach, the ankles of the wearer. The band cincture worn by CECO's clergy is 4-6 inches in width terminating in a fringe[6] on both ends. Covering the cassock the adjutant who has been ordained an elder shall don the white Roman (square-yoked) surplice. This surplice shall reach the knees of the wearer and shall bear pleats down the front and back as its sole adornment.

The Clerical attire for the **adjutant** who has been appointed an **Overseer** shall be the same as that of the ordained elder. During gatherings of the fellowship the overseer shall don his fuchsia adjutants cord.

The Liturgical attire for the **adjutant** who has been appointed an **Overseer** shall be the black Roman cassock with matching band cincture, white rochet with pleated cuffs (black bands) and a black chimere. The Overseer shall also make use of the black tippet, denoting jurisdiction within the scope of his appointment. The overseer may also wear the silver episcopal ring bearing CECO's seal on his right hand ring finger. This is optional.

Regular Clergy

The Clerical attire for **licentiates** of CECO is a plain black suit, black hosiery, black shoes and a black tab collar shirt. Liturgical attire for licentiates shall be a black Roman cassock.

---

[6] Fringe is not to be confused with tassels. A fringe consists of short threads; a tassel is a bunch of threads fastened together at one end.

Deacons shall wear a plain black suit, black hosiery, black shoes and a black neckband shirt with the "brothers" Collarette affixed. Liturgical attire for deacons is the plain white front-wrap alb.

The Clerical attire for **Elders** of the Fellowship shall be a plain black suit, black hosiery, black shoes, black cord[7] with a silver cross no more than 3" in height and black neckband shirt with white Roman collar. Liturgical attire for Elders is the black Roman cassock with matching band cincture, black cord and silver cross. The band cincture worn by Elders shall terminate in fringe and be 4-6" in width.

Senior Pastors of the churches of the Fellowship shall wear the same clerical attire as ordained elders with the addition of the black and gold pastor's cord to accompany their silver cross no more than 3" in height. In like fashion, the Liturgical attire for the Senior Pastors shall be the same as the ordained Elder with the addition of the white Roman Surplice. This surplice may be adorned with a tasteful application of lace at the hem and sleeves if so desired by the pastor

Overseers of the Fellowship shall be adorned in the plain black suit with black hosiery, black shoes and a black neckband shirt with white Roman collar for their clerical attire. Further, Overseers shall also make use of the scarlet cross-cord and silver pectoral cross. Concerning liturgical attire, as the sixth order of prelature, the Overseer shall make use of the white rochet with black banded (and pleated) cuffs and the black chimere. In addition, Overseers are authorized the use of the black tippet with the Seal of the Fellowship on the left panel. Lastly, at the discretion of the prelate, the Overseer may wear the silver episcopal ring bearing the Seal of the Fellowship on the ring finger of their right hand.

General Overseers shall make the use of the gray neckband shirt for their clerical attire. Further, the General Overseers of this Fellowship shall utilize the silver chain from which suspends their silver pectoral cross for their Episcopal jewelry as well as the episcopal ring bearing the Seal of the Fellowship. The liturgical attire for General Overseers is the same as prescribed for Overseers, with the exception of the

---

[7] All cords authorized for wear by CECO clergy shall be 38" in length. When in Civic attire the cross shall be placed in the left breast pocket of the wearer.

aforementioned silver chain for these officers which shall be no shorter in length than 40".

Consecrated **Bishops** of the Fellowship shall wear either the blue-purple or red-purple neckband shirt while dressed in clerical attire, at the date of this manual's publication, the choice remains theirs. Episcopal jewelry may also be worn by these prelates in the form of the gold chain no less than 40" in length and the gold pectoral cross. The Episcopal ring bearing an amethyst stone is also a part of the jewelry of the prelate. Those prelates who are also primates over their own Reformations may wear the red neckband shirt during gatherings of CECO at the discretion of our Presiding Prelate. As a matter of protocol and deference to the Presiding Prelate of this Fellowship, other prelates shall not wear the red breast front when the Presiding Prelate is similarly dressed. Only when our Primate is wearing a white breast front shall the red be worn by others. This is an unspoken rule among episcopates and simply shows due respect to the office of the Presiding Prelate of this Fellowship.

For Liturgical attire, the prelates of this Fellowship shall wear the black Roman cassock, Bishop's cincture, white rochet with fuchsia wristbands, blue purple chimere, black tippet, fuchsia zucchetto and fuchsia biretta and all episcopal jewelry.

The Choir dress for Bishops of this Fellowship shall consist of the chianti Roman cassock, fuchsia cincture terminating in tassels (also known as the Bishop's Cincture), white rochet with chianti wristbands, chianti chimere, and tippet. Finally, the bishops shall wear the fuchsia zucchetto and the fuchsia biretta with episcopal jewelry.

ENDNOTES AND BIBLIOGRAPHY

ENDNOTES

Chapter I
DISCIPLESHIP

1. Godin, S. (2008). *Tribes: We Need You To Lead Us.* London: Penguin Books

2. Dake, F. L. (2011). *Dake's Annotated Reference Bible.* Lawrenceville: Dake Bible Sales Inc.

3. www.as.org

4. Foster, R. J. (1976). *Celebration of Discipline: The Path to Spiritual Growth.* San Francisco: Harper Collins.

5. Schaeffer, F. A. (1976). *How Shall We Then Live: The Rise and Decline of Western Thought.* Wheaton: Crossway Books.

6. Ibid.

7. Damazio, F. (1988). *The Making of a Leader.* Portland: City Bible Publishing.

8. Foster, R. J. (1976). *Celebration of Discipline: The Path to Spiritual Growth.* San Francisco: Harper Collins.

9. Ibid.

10. Ibid.

11. Ibid.

Chapter II
WHAT IS AN ADJUTANT

1. Merriam-Webster, Incorporated. (2002). *Merriam-Webster's Collegiate Dictionary.* Springfield: Merriam-Webster, Incorporated

2. Ellis II, J. D. (2006). *Vocati Ad Ministrandum* Trafford Publishing, p. 6.

3. Ibid.

4. Srtong, James. (1995). *Strong's Exhaustive Concordance of the Bible.* Nashville: Thomas Nelson Publishers

5. Ibid.

6. Ibid.

7. Peat, Jr., A. A. & Stevens, D. J. (2013) *Famulus de Episcopo.* Columbia: CECO Publishing. p.16.

Chapter III
THE SERVANT MINISTRY OF ADJUTANTS

1. Ellis II, J. D. (2006). *Vocati Ad Ministrandum* Trafford Publishing, p.19.

2. Ibid., p.24.

3. Ibid., p.9.

Endnotes and Bibliography

Chapter IV
EPISCOPAL ORDERS

1. Ellis II, J. D. (2003). *The Bishopric*. Bloomington: Trafford Publishing. p.24.

2. Ibid., p.27.

3. Ibid., p.29.

4. Rook, P. (1907). *Auxiliary Bishop*. Retrieved from The Catholic Encyclopedia: http://www.newadvent.org/cathen/02145b.htm

5. Ellis II, J. D. (2003). *The Bishopric*. Bloomington: Trafford Publishing. p.30.

6. Ibid., p.24.

7. Ibid., p.31

Chapter V
EPISCOPAL INSIGNIA

1. Merriam-Webster, Incorporated. (2002). *Merriam-Webster's Collegiate Dictionary*. Springfield: Merriam-Webster, Incorporated

2. James-Charles Noonan, J. (1996). *The Church Visible: The Ceremonial Life and Protocol of the Roman Catholic Church*. New York: Viking Penguin, p.286.

3. Merriam-Webster, Incorporated. (2002). *Merriam-Webster's Collegiate Dictionary*. Springfield: Merriam-Webster, Incorporated

Chapter VI
EPISCOPAL VESTMENTS

1. Walsh, J. (1909). *The Mass and Vestments of the Catholic Church*. Troy: Troy Times Art Press, p.424.

2. Ibid.

3. James-Charles Noonan, J. (1996). *The Church Visible: The Ceremonial Life and Protocol of the Roman Catholic Church*. New York: Viking Penguin, p.286.

4. Ibid., p.298.

5. Nainfa, J. A. (1926). *Costume of the Prelates of the Catholic Church According to Roman Etiquette* Baltimore: John Murphy Company, p.68.

6. Merriam-Webster, Incorporated. (2002). *Merriam-Webster's Collegiate Dictionary*. Springfield: Merriam-Webster, Incorporated

7. James-Charles Noonan, J. (1996). *The Church Visible: The Ceremonial Life and Protocol of the Roman Catholic Church*. New York: Viking Penguin, p.299.

8. Walsh, J. (1909). *The Mass and Vestments of the Catholic Church*. Troy: Troy Times Art Press, p.424.

9. James-/harles Noonan, J. (1996). *The Church Visible: The Ceremonial Life and Protocol of the Roman Catholic Church*. New York: Viking Penguin, p.365.

10. Nainfa, J. A. (1926). *Costume of the Prelates of the Catholic Church According to Roman Etiquette* Baltimore: John Murphy Company, p.13.

Chapter VII
ECCLESIASTICAL PROTOCOL AND
ETIQUETTE

1. Merriam-Webster, Incorporated. (2002). *Merriam-Webster's Collegiate Dictionary.* Springfield: Merriam-Webster, Incorporated.

2. Ibid.

BIBLIOGRAPHY

Ahaus, H. (1911). Holy Orders. In The Catholic Encyclopedia. New York: Robert Appleton Company. Retrieved March 28, 2013 from New Advent: http://www.newadvent.org/cathen/11279a.htm

Boudinhon, A. (1911). Primate. In The Catholic Encyclopedia. New York: Robert Appleton Company. Retrieved March 28, 2013 from New Advent: http://www.newadvent.org/cathen/12423b.htm

Ellis II, J. D. (2003). *The Bishopric.* Bloomington: Trafford Publishing.

Ellis II, J. D. (2006). *Vocati Ad Ministrandum.* Bloomington: Trafford Publishing.

James-Charles Noonan, J. (1996). *The Church Visible: The Ceremonial Life and Protocol of the Roman Catholic Church.* New York: Viking Penguin.

Knight, K. (2009). *The Catholic Encyclopedia.* Retrieved Aug 23, 2011, from New Advent: http://www.newadvent.org/cathen/index.html

Merriam-Webster, Incorporated. (2002). *Merriam-Webster's Collegiate Dictionary.* Springfield: Merriam-Webster, Incorperated.

Nainfa, J. A. (1926). *Costume of Prelates of the Catholic Church According to Roman Etiquette.* Baltimore: John Murphy Company.

Peat, A., & Stevens, D. (2012). *Famulus de Episcopo: An Adjutant's Manual.* Columbia: CECO Publishing.

Rook, P. (1907). *Auxiliary Bishop.* Retrieved from The Catholic Encyclopedia: http://www.newadvent.org/cathen/02145b.htm

Schofield, C. I. (Ed.). (1909). *The Schofield Study Bible* (King James Version ed.). New York, New York, United States: Oxford University Press.

Vatican Ecumenical Council. (1989). *Ceremonial of Bishops.* Collegeville: The Liturgical Press.

Walsh, J. (1909). *The Mass and Vestments of the Catholic Church.* Troy: Troy Times Art Press.

About the Authors

About the Authors

Bishop Arnulfo Aurelio Peat, Jr.

Bishop Arnulfo Aurelio Peat, Jr. is a native of Brooklyn, New York, and currently resides in Columbia, Missouri. Bishop Peat is a well-respected teacher of the Word, specializing in leadership and church development. His teaching is known as being intellectually challenging and charismatic. Peat is the founder of Christian Cultural International Ministries (CCIM), along with his wife Nicole Peat, whose purpose is to go into every man's world; encouraging, teaching, and challenging the hearts and minds of individuals with the empowering message of the Gospel of Jesus Christ.

Bishop Peat began his journey in ministry in 1992, while attending the University of Wisconsin-Madison, under the leadership of Pastor Lemont R. Sherrill, Watch Force Ministries. There he was appointed a deacon and later that year during a prayer meeting accepted his calling into ministry. September 1993, Peat received his license of ministry and became an Associate Pastor. On October 15, 1994, Peat became an ordained minister under Pastor Lawrence Ware, where Bishop Russell L. Freeman participated in Peat being set apart to the Gospel. Bishop A. Peat, Jr. served as pastor of New Covenant Church of Christ in Madison, Wisconsin for a season. Bishop Russell L. Freeman has been a Spiritual Father from the very beginning and has watched over Arnulfo A. Peat, Jr. since 1992. Peat has served in various capacities under the leadership of Bishop R.L. Freeman since 1995. Arnulfo A. Peat currently serves on the ministry team of United Community Cathedral. Arnulfo A. Peat is one of the Founding Fathers of Christians Equipping Christians for Outreach (CECO), where he serves administratively in CECO's Apostolic See.

Bishop A.A. Peat, Jr. has earned degrees from University of Wisconsin-Madison, William Woods University, and has done graduate studies at Oral Roberts University in The School of Education.

Peat has been an educator with Columbia Public Schools for over ten year. Bishop Peat developed the "Aspiring Scholars" curriculum, for which in 2009, he was awarded "The Most Outstanding Educator of the Year in a Specialized Area" (specifically for his work in closing the achievement gap of minority students). He challenges students to develop character, leadership skills, and to believe in their gifts and talents.

Bishop Peat's wife, Nicole, is his partner in ministry, business, and purpose. They are proud parents and leading a legacy for their three children: Elisha, Nathaniel, and Valerie Peat.

Elder David Stevens

Elder David Stevens was born on February 10, 1979 in Fairfax, VA to Bishop Michael M. and Lady Andrea R. Stevens. It was in 2005, amid the isolated deserts of Iraq that his ministry while Overseer Stevens served as a Staff Sergeant in the Marines. Shortly after that tour was over, the Marine Corps saw fit to reassign Brother Stevens to duty at Fort Leonard Wood, Missouri to instruct at its engineer school. It was here in 2008, that Brother Stevens found a mentor in Bishop Willie J. Curry (Senior Pastor of Shekinah Tabernacle Ministries). Bishop Curry recognized Brother Stevens' servant's heart and accepted him as his armor bearer. While serving under the guidance and tutelage of Bishop Curry, Minister Stevens was licensed and later, in 2009, ordained by Shekinah Tabernacle Ministries of St. Robert, Mo.

After ordination, Elder Stevens continued to faithfully serve as adjutant to Bishop Curry but the Lord had more for him as his exposure to the apostolic expanded with his introduction to Christians Equipping Christians for Outreach Fellowship, Inc. (CECO). During the summer of 2010, with the blessing of his Senior Pastor, Elder Stevens moved from the membership of Shekinah and came under the spiritual covering of CECO. It was soon thereafter, by the leading of the Holy Spirit, that Elder Stevens and family joined in ministry with United Community Cathedral of Columbia, Mo. where Bishop Russell L. Freeman is the Senior Pastor and Senior Bishop.

In the autumn of 2010, while serving at *United*, Elder Stevens' zeal for order and his servant's heart were again exposed, and he was appointed Adjutant to His Grace, Bishop Herman D. Ware, Jr., a post that he continues to occupy today with much love, service, loyalty and enjoyment. From his appointment as adjutant to Bishop Ware, Elder Stevens was caused to expand in ministry and spiritual awareness. It was here in *United* that Elder Stevens realized his love for serving people and especially God's leaders as the Lord allowed his servant's heart to flourish. In the summer of 2011, Elder Stevens began to serve *United* as the Director of

Protocol and Adjutancy, promoting Ecclesiastical Order and instructing in protocol and etiquette. As God's plan continued to unfold for Elder Stevens, in the same year he was appointed Dean of CECO's School of Adjutancy where he promotes uniformity and the Spirit of discipleship amongst the National Fellowship.

After 14 long years of faithful and enjoyable service to his country and the Marine Corps, Elder Stevens once again heeded the call of his Lord and made the decision to forgo the six short years to retirement, to instead step out in faith. In the winter of 2011, Elder Stevens exited the Marine Corps with an Honorable Discharge as a Gunnery Sergeant of Marines in order to stay under the direct leadership of Bishop Freeman, and the mentorship of Bishop Ware. God honored Elder Stevens' faithfulness and continued to pull ministry out of him and propel him forward. In time, Elder Stevens was appointed an Overseer of Protocol by the hand of Bishop Russell L. Freeman of United Community Cathedral. Elder Stevens currently serves as Adjutant to Bishop H.D. Ware Jr., Overseer of Protocol and Adjutancy in United Community Cathedral, and Dean of the School of Adjutancy for CECO.

He is married to the lovely LaToya D. Stevens of 15 years and together they have four active, unique and adventurous sons: David II, Marcus, Matthew and Nathaniel.

98 | About the Authors

www.ingramcontent.com/pod-product-compliance
Lightning Source LLC
Chambersburg PA
CBHW022109160426
43198CB00008B/402